JOURNEY
TO
POLAND
AND
YUGOSLAVIA

JOURNEY

TO

POLAND

AND

YUGOSLAVIA

JOHN KENNETH GALBRAITH

HARVARD UNIVERSITY PRESS

Cambridge, Massachusetts

1958

Library of Congress Catalogue Card Number 58–14482

Printed in the United States of America

Foreword

In the spring of 1958 I was invited by the University of Warsaw and the Polish Economic Society to give a series of lectures on economics and the American economy. The Ford Foundation, through the Institute of International Education, arranged for the journey. Subsequently, Professor Janez Stanovnik of the Institute of International Politics and Economics asked me to extend my trip to Yugoslavia. This was — at least so I was told — the first comprehensive series of lectures on capitalism to be given by a nonsocialist in any Communist country since the Russian revolution.

I have, I imagine, at least a normal curiosity as to how other economic systems function. I am also persuaded that far more problems in economic behavior are common to capitalist and socialist or Communist countries than we commonly allow ourselves to suppose. The cliché has it that these economies are as different as day from night. In truth there are many similarities; and more differences

v

than we think are to be explained by tradition, geography and, above all, by levels of past well-being and present development.

For all these reasons I kept careful diary notes of my movements, observations, and conversations, and on my return I had them mimeographed for circulation to my friends. This led to the suggestion that they be published.

While I had written the notes without such thought, I did not resist very hard. Much of the joy of traveling has always been in telling of it thereafter. But Americans now do so much traveling that one can often find an audience only by paying heed in turn to the pedestrian or improbable reports of his friends. Accordingly, one cherishes the chance to tell without having to listen.

A diary, it is perhaps worth pointing out, is not a definitive tract. No doubt there is some rule against setting down pure nonsense. But part of its purpose is to record comment that the visitor hears as he hears it and to record impressions as he forms them. The reader knows from the context that he should frequently reserve judgment. So it is with this chronology, and where the ground seems especially shaky I have added a special warning.

Various people have suggested that, since I refer frequently to my lectures in this account, I should reproduce them. The difficulty is that they were not very new: they covered ground which I had been over before with American readers and with my students. Although the publishing industry is sustained by authors who are busily plagiarizing themselves, this is not defensible as a premeditated crime. I have compromised by including one lecture — the one which, at least as a synthesis and summary, had the best claim to interest. It deals, among other things, with the notion of countervailing power to which I had been particularly requested to address myself.

I have generally avoided quoting by name my Polish and Yugoslav sources in this account. This is not because I have any great fear of compromising them. Many people in both countries take no small pride in speaking plainly and do so without evident restraint. Rather, those with whom I talked had no reason to suppose that I would quote them, and I had no thought of doing so when we talked. Therefore, it has seemed a matter of common politeness to be sparing with names.

J. K. G.

Cambridge, Massachusetts
September 1958

CONTENTS

JOURNEY

TO

POLAND

AND

YUGOSLAVIA

Paris to Warsaw

May 8, 1958

I left Paris this morning at eight forty-five, having arisen at six, and I have often felt better. Paris never seemed so lovely as it was last night, and in good company I postponed all but completely going to bed. It was a gay and even enchanting night at the price of a rather poor morning.

My plane, a KLM Viscount, was in Amsterdam in a little more than an hour, and we circled the city before landing. The canals glistened in the sun. So did the city.

At Amsterdam airport I received the disconcerting news that although my reservations had been confirmed — as my ticket fortunately showed — I was not on the passenger list for Warsaw. Moreover, the plane, a KLM Constellation, was full. I was told that someone might fail to show up, and I was thus comforted until a few minutes before departure, when I was informed with many expressions of regret that everyone was on hand. (The travelers were Poles returning from visits abroad.) I carried an appeal to the manager and pointed out that I was traveling KLM because of its reliability. I also pictured the reception committee that would be awaiting my arrival at Warsaw and, drawing somewhat on my imagination, I said there might even be a press conference. After further delay and much negotiation, I was made a paying member of the crew and ascended to the compartment behind the flight deck. We circled from Amsterdam around through Denmark to avoid the forbidden territory of East Germany, and my spirits were improved by a large whisky. We came low into Warsaw over villages which, as in French Canada, string out endlessly along the roads making a continuous line of houses. Behind each dwelling is a ribbon of land a mile or so long and little wider than the house. It is a convivial but inefficient design.

At Warsaw I was welcomed warmly by a delegation from the university and the Polish Economic Society. An agreeable and very good-looking girl customs guard said, "How are you? May I just glance at your currency declaration?" She then waved to a porter to pick up my bags and we were on our way to town.

The Warsaw airport is a shabby and dreary place even on a spring day. The buildings are of temporary one-story construction and resemble those of a war-time air base. And the trip into the city is no improvement on that from Newark. Warsaw, the planners notwithstanding, suffers from a bad case of urban sprawl — the sprawl in this case taking the form of large blocks of apartments which stand around seemingly at random. The best are ungainly and the worst are ugly, and the ugliness is heightened by the building material which is poor or reconditioned brick. As one gets closer to town the war damage becomes evident; in large areas it is still oppressive. One passes through the part of the city from which the Germans evacuated all of the population in the closing days of the occupation.

I am lodged at the Grand Hotel ORBIS — ORBIS is the official tourist agency — which, like everything else in Warsaw, is still being completed. The rooms are small but adequate and are furnished in Sears-Grand Rapids. Someone supplied me with four nice tulips. Since state property is involved, there is an inventory of all the artifacts tacked on the cupboard door.

I had scarcely time for a bath before two economists from the university — one of them associated with the Planning Board — arrived for a chat. They told me of the controversy going on over the question of centralization versus decentralization of the economy. This does not involve the issue of social ownership of land and capital which, though it has been given up for agriculture, is not in debate elsewhere. Rather it is whether production will be in accordance with a comprehensive, centrally-formulated plan covering both investment and current production decisions, or whether the state, while retaining some control of investment, will allow considerable autonomy to the individual firm, especially in its production decisions. These would be subject to guidance by the market. Both my visitors were ardent decentralizers.

Presently one of my visitors observed that I was tired and then I had a couple of hours' sleep. Thereafter I was met by officials of the Polish Economic Society, and we walked through downtown Warsaw to a good dinner preceded by several rounds of vodka which I was encouraged to toss off at a single gulp. I felt very traveled. Visitors to Russia, I know from many accounts, are always knocking off vodka at a gulp.

Our dinner conversation ranged over a great number of subjects, but mostly it had to do with the state of the Polish economy. "Since October" recurred constantly in the conversation and this, of course, refers to the retreat of the Stalinists and the reëmergence of Gomulka in October 1956. "Since October," in the view of my hosts, the position of the peasants has improved as has the efficiency of Polish agriculture. But the situation of the urban population is not much better — certainly it has not improved in accordance with expectations. There is more than a little frustration and discouragement. Much is blamed on the "bureaucracy" — on the conservatism and reluctance of the party and the administrators in tackling needed reforms. "Our price system is idiotic," one of my hosts observed, "and nothing is being done about it." A second agreed, although he was less pessimistic about the prospects for improvement. Both said that the unhappy position of the urban workers and intellectuals had elements of danger. "The most articulate people are suffering most."

Incidentally, the vodka led to a discussion of alcoholism, which is very serious in Poland. One of my hosts produced an interesting economic explanation. In an economy where consumer's goods are not plentiful, where private investment is difficult, and where savings have been repeatedly eroded by inflation, there are few outlets for extra funds. But they can always be plowed into alcohol.

On the way home I asked if it was not true that the standard of living in Poland is higher than in the Soviet Union, averaging country with city and developed regions with more primitive ones. My hosts thought that it was. I then asked why people talked so much about the Polish economic problem and so little about the Russian economic problem. It was agreed that this was an interesting question and also that the answer was easy. The Poles have learned to want a great deal more.

Warsaw: First Impressions

May 9

Last night I inquired of the ORBIS girl on my floor
— she serves as interpreter and counselor to the
guests on the floor — where I might get some shirts
washed. She told me to collect and bring them, and
this morning before I was up the phone rang and
she was inquiring whether the maid might bring
them in. There they were, sparkling white and
cleaner than the Harvard *Coop* ever got them. I
was still reflecting on the relative efficiency of these
two socialist laundry establishments later in the
morning when the ORBIS girl told me that I should
pay the chambermaid separately. The hotel laundry
will not be operating for another two months, and
meantime the maids are doing the laundry on their
own time. It is Polish private enterprise that is better
than Cambridge socialism.

I had breakfast in the new hotel dining room. It is
a pleasant although vaguely conventional, slightly
too-cushioned room. It was full of people talking in

whispers or low voices in a rather conspiratorial way. Behind me were three sinister-looking men who were whispering in English. Presently I heard one of them say, "He has real courage. He wouldn't hesitate to get fired to help us." I decided to listen. But eventually I discovered that they were discussing the chances of chiropractors getting recognition from the regular medical practitioners in Cleveland, Ohio.

After breakfast I went for a long walk through downtown Warsaw to the Hotel Bristol, the headquarters of ORBIS, where I changed some money. Most of the downtown section of Warsaw has been rebuilt in a rather severe style, emphasizing vertical lines and windows. It is much criticized — indeed, last night one of my hosts pointed to some trees in a square and noted that they were a concession to the critics of "social realism" in architecture. However, my path this morning was along a street which recaptures the style of the prewar city. It is varied and quite pleasant.

The skyline of Warsaw is dominated by the *Palac Kultury i Nauki* (Palace of Culture and Science), a gift of the Soviet Union. This is a skyscraper of some thirty stories, and it soars incredibly in a city where scarcely another building is more than ten. The Palace does not reflect the influence of "social real-

8

ism," but it is startlingly reminiscent of the Woolworth Building. The proportions are less satisfactory.

There is not much traffic on the streets, although the city has a lively aspect. A few of the women are smart in appearance; many more are good looking. But most of the women and all of the men are a trifle shabby. One senses that respectability requires a good deal of effort and improvisation. The shops are austere by Western standards, although I saw some interesting bookstores, and one department store had a large and lethal-looking inventory of red motorcycles. A solitary pushcart peddler was selling two grades of apples, both rather underprivileged, at Z10 and Z14 a kilo. At the tourist rate the zloty is about four cents.

On the way I noticed an old woman with a broom of sticks sweeping the streets. For many years I have been reading about these women and, at long last, I felt that I had made spiritual contact with the Slavic world. I also reflected that having old women sweep the streets is greatly inferior to our system of not sweeping them at all.

After supplying myself with some money, I went to the embassy where I chatted with Jacob Beam, our ambassador, and later with members of his staff. Agricultural aid came up. In the last year, or a little more, we have supplied the Poles with about 1.1

million tons of bread and feed grain. The Russians have supplied some 1.7 million tons. Perhaps Poland is not to be forever victimized by its geography.

I lunched by myself at the Grand Hotel ORBIS and not without difficulty persuaded the headwaiter that I would like a drink. Eventually I received a small tumblerful of vodka. It substantially quickens the perceptions.

At three I called by appointment on an old acquaintance who is now a high official in the Planning Ministry. He seemed pleased with the rather technical economic volume — Dorfman, Samuelson, and Solow on *Linear Programming*[1] — that I brought him, and for a while we conversed amicably enough. He is working on long-range planning problems — problems beyond the present plan — and told me that in his view the rate of investment is limited not by the supply of savings but by the amount of investment, and in particular of construction, that can be administered at any time. This capacity to administer investment is the ultimate bottleneck. I pressed him as to whether it was one which investment itself — i.e., in supervisory personnel — could break. He expressed doubts. Nor did he think decentralization was a remedy. The latter, he argued, was largely a function of the supply of resources. The easier the supply the more one can decentralize administration and risk waste. The fewer the resources, the greater the need to control by centralized administration. He pointed, as an example, to the centralization of authority over resources which wartime scarcities forced upon the United States. He told me that the present objective is to bring living standards in Poland up to the level of such Western European countries as Holland or Denmark by 1970. This is a formidable goal.

Thereafter our discussion deteriorated into an argument over the United States economy. He kept referring to the decisive role of arms expenditures. I pointed out that in relation to GNP, government spending was not vastly greater than in 1939 and that, besides military outlays, state and local spending had risen rapidly. He refuted me with some recalculations of national income involving concepts which I could not follow. In the end I gave up.

After a tour to take some pictures — nothing very interesting — I went to dinner with the leading members of the Polish Economic Society. On the way, my guide (a young and vigorously anti-Stalinist instructor) and I were caught in a violent thunderstorm. We took refuge in a coffee bar, and he asked me whether Americans preferred small coffee shops or large ones. While I was wondering if I should explain about bars, taverns, and saloons we heard,

11

along with the crash of thunder, the sound of bugles and drums. A parade of soldiers and some boy scouts came bravely along through the cloudburst.

"I think it may be some visiting delegation," said my guide hopefully. But it wasn't, and the drenched marchers disappeared in the downpour.

The dinner was good and lively, but I learned little, for I was asked questions — many of them about United States agriculture. In consequence, all my normal tendencies notwithstanding, I talked rather than listened.

There was more critical discussion of the economic plan. "No country has done so much for the theory of planning as Poland and so little for the practice."

I walked home with one of my hosts by the vast party headquarters, and he discussed the curious duality of the party and the ministerial government. Some important ministers are not members of the United Workers' or Communist Party, yet they are obviously responsible in the immediate sense for a large number of decisions. Where does their authority end and where does that of the party begin? How much negotiation between party official and minister must precede any action? There seems no doubt that it is an awkward and time-consuming way of making decisions. Yet it is worth recalling that

12

most government procedures are awkward. We regularly defend awkwardness as the democratic way.

Other questions of the evening: How much is the American economy dependent on arms? Did the Sputniks accelerate the arms race?

Tour of Warsaw

May 10

This morning I was taken on a long tour of Warsaw. My guide was an intelligent young engineer who supplements his earnings by taking visitors around. We saw the Belvedere Palace, the vast new Soviet Embassy — a showy and tasteless neo-classical structure in great unkempt grounds — the former royal park, and the old city. The central square in the old city, though it was completely destroyed, has been reconstructed in the original form. The result is exceedingly plausible and a great source of pride to everyone. The nearby cathedral is also being rebuilt by the government, although without some unsatisfactory features added in the nineteenth century. Catholic cathedral building in a Communist country by a Communist government sets in motion some interesting reflections. There is also, I discover, considerable pride in such anomalies.

Eventually we came to the site of the ghetto. This is northwest of the old city, and into this area the

Germans herded the Jewish population — some four hundred thousand in all — and surrounded them with the famous wall. From here people were deported to the death camps until the hopeless uprising of 1943. Then men, women, and children were burned and slaughtered *en situ,* and all the buildings were leveled to the ground. The place is still a desert of weeds and rubble, and the smell of death still seems to hang over it. Even in the sunshine of a bright spring morning it is altogether hideous.

I then went with my guide to the top of the Soviet-built *Palac Kultury i Nauki.* Like the embassy, it is meant to impress but succeeds in being unimaginative, ornate, and lacking in finish. Where Rockefeller Center is elegant, this is somehow rather crude and awkward. However, the school children who were also visiting it were better pleased than I. Moreover, I think my guide was impressed too. It is very, very high and must seem so to a Polish youngster. From the top there is an excellent view of Warsaw west of the Vistula and likewise of the still unredeemed devastation. My guide suggested that complete rebuilding will not be finished for another ten years.

I went to lunch with the Beams, the party including the Joe Harsches and Flora Gruson, the well-informed wife of the equally attractive and well-

informed correspondent of the *New York Times*.
Very pleasant, and we talked about everyone's favorite subject, namely Poland, until mid-afternoon.
These are days of great delicacy in the Polish position, with the government attempting to walk a
thin line which avoids Titoist heresy on the one hand
and keeps an open window westward on the other.
The press has been severely limited in recent weeks.
The universities remain relatively free (a matter of
some immediate personal interest), and the secret
police have not been reactivated following their sup-
pression or restriction in 1956. The church also remains relatively untroubled. All makes for endlessly
interesting discussion. However, I am always a trifle
uneasy about such conversation. It is excessively preoccupied with the meaning of the mood and events
of the moment — with things that will be forgotten
a month hence. And in this discussion of tactics the
questions of strategy, of the larger framework, are in-
variably ignored. We watch to see who is out of step.
We never see where the troops are marching.

I had a nap and then joined Calvin Hoover,[1] who
is visiting here briefly, and three Polish economists
for tea. One of them, the professor of econometrics,
was enchanted with a copy of Dorfman, Samuelson,
and Solow and kept leafing through its complex
pages. He told us that since Gomulka econometrics,

and especially linear programming, have been made legal in Poland. (The Stalinists may have had something.) I gave a copy of Edward S. Mason's recently published essays[2] to another economist who works on the role of the state in the capitalist countries. She hurriedly glanced at it to assure herself that it contained no mathematical symbols, and then expressed her pleasure.

We then had a general discussion turning on this problem: Prior to Gomulka's coming to power the government and party had claimed a steady rise in both total output and in consumers' goods. On taking power in 1956, Gomulka had said that this improvement, so far as the consumer was concerned, was fictitious. What lay back of these initially misleading conclusions? While this question was not asked, it was implicity in the question whether the figures had been faked.

Two answers were suggested. First and most important, inventories were being accumulated rather than being passed on to the consumer. This accumulation was very high. And armament production was also high, and these inedibles were apparently included in the total of final goods. Secondly, the totals were swollen by goods of such low quality that they added nothing to living standards. They were unusable or unsalable but were in the statistics nonetheless. This observation confirms one made by Oskar Lange[3] in 1956.

We then discussed whether an economy like that of Poland should adjust output and income by moving prices or wages. The Russians change prices; the disposition of the Poles is to act on wages. It is a nice point. I should suppose that if output is growing the most nearly neutral step is reduce prices. (Wage adjustments will always involve some alterations in the relative wage structure.) And I would assume that this method would be most conducive to saving. I imagine that it also involves difficulties where, as in Poland, the agriculture is not socialized.

We talked in the restaurant of the hotel, which was full of fairly well-dressed people who were having ice cream or tea and listening to Strauss waltzes and Hungarian songs.

A final note: The local economists were most anxious to have a draft of my lectures that it might be reproduced. Now I learn that they are not to be reproduced. I am anxious as to the reason.

Visit to the Country

May 11

I am told the problem is one of finding a typist who could deal with English — "a formidable technical problem when faced." So be it.

Today was fascinating. At 9:30 I departed Warsaw to Lowicz, some eighty kilometers to the west. I had as guides two agricultural experts, one a merry stump of a man with an enormous mustache and a plausible resemblance to Captain Kidd. A young member of the university came along as a translator. My piratical friend told me that in prewar Poland he had helped introduce the 4-H Clubs. He inquired if they were still functioning in the United States. I reassured him and told him they continued to contribute their mite to our surplus. He also told me how, over peasant resistance, he had introduced fertilizer in the highly conservative villages where he had worked. At night he spread fertilizer on the growing fields in the form of a cross. When the priest was unable to explain the miracle, he stepped in. He

19

asked me if I were a Catholic, and when I told him that I was not he went on to observe that Polish peasants were perversely willing to spend more money on their salvation in the next world than in this.

On the way we stopped to visit a seat of the Radziwill family, who ruled in Poland from the Middle Ages and survived to the end of World War II (the last Radziwill left with the Germans in 1945 and returned to be picked up by the Russians. A brother has managed better and is now in the Foreign Ministry.) It is an interesting but not especially inviting chateau. The most interesting piece of furniture is a harmonium made of tuned glass tumblers.

Next we went to church. On the road we had seen numerous people standing outside the churches which our guide said were too crowded to accommodate all clients. This one, of cathedral size and gaily decorated for a wedding in white flowers and ribbons, was also overflowing. Nearly all the men were participating from the churchyard. The church itself was a breath-taking sight. The women were nearly all in local folk costume with brilliant white and rose scarves on their heads. The singing was even more wonderful. It was some sort of responsive hymn, and the sound rose and was reflected from the high reaches of the Gothic arches. I do not expect to hear anything quite to match it again. It was clear, spirited, and in some unidentifiable way, magnificent. My friend from the university was also deeply impressed. "I had no idea anything like this was to be heard in Poland."

My pirate friend went into the church to snap a few pictures. He told me that, "as a fellow pagan," I could do the same. I couldn't help noticing that my "fellow pagan" kneeled and crossed himself with some care once he was inside. Then he took his pictures.

After the wedding I also took pictures. The women were beautifully garbed and posed without excessive reluctance. The results may well put the *National Geographic* to shame.

Next we went to an agricultural school for lunch. The latter—tomato soup with sour cream, pork cutlets, potatoes, and cake — was very good. Next I said a few avuncular words to some of the students (boarding students of high-school age) and we went on to visit a village. This was the high spot of the day. We were guided by a growing body of villagers who marveled at my height and bickered over my exact metric dimensions. We went, finally, to one of the larger houses for tea, beer, sausage, and cakes, and an hour or two of discussion.

The talk was exceedingly free and made me think

21

U. S. cattlemen might be easier to collectivize. "We survived under the czars, we survived under the Germans, we survived under the Stalinists, and we will continue to survive," one of them told me adding, "We tell the officials just what we tell you." Since two officials were present this seemed likely. I asked them if they were happy now and they replied that, on the whole, they were. Income is increasing, there is money to invest and there are building materials to buy. Individual farmers in the village have acquired six tractors in recent weeks.

This village was never collectivized, and the holdings were always rather small. Accordingly, the land reform which here sets a limit of sixteen hectares (about forty acres) has had but little effect. However, my host had had a few more acres than the limit and had been labeled a kulak. It still rankled. "Is that a name to call me; do I look like a dangerous man? I was so angry I just sat in my house."

Now kulaks are no more. There is still a machine and tractor station in the vicinity, but the villagers do not use it. "You cannot get the work done at the proper time." Fertilizer, which was long scarce, is available in adequate quantity. The compulsory deliveries at less than market prices plus the heavy land taxes — about forty dollars a hectare calculated at the tourist rate — are still sources of complaint. But, as compared with the Stalinist period, the position is fairly favorable. They made a point of telling me that because of the relatively high cultural level of the village there was no alcoholism. Someone asked me if alcoholism was now a problem in the farm villages of the United States. I told them that while in the cities our people drank too much, in the country it was the other way around.

My questions frequently provoked long debates over answers, but it was a merry party. They asked me the size of the farm on which I was born. When I told them 150 acres, they said, "Oh, you *were* indeed kulaks." When I slowed down on the cake and sausages, my host said, "You must fulfill your plan."

On the way home we were stopped for speeding, and it also developed that our car did not have the required first-aid kit. But the driver told the policeman that he had an "American professor" aboard. The cop put his head in the window, looked me over, and then waved us on. A wise and discriminatory system of law enforcement.

Tonight I had dinner with Harold Linder,[1] Calvin Hoover, and Douglass Cater and wife.[2] We talked as usual about the Polish economy. The feeling of Americans about socialism seems to me quite a lot like that toward sex. There is deep fascination, a desire to look, and if possible to touch, but no desire to become involved.

Lecture

May 12

A further note on the villages and the agricultural scene. In the late forties the government started the intensive collectivization drive, and a considerable proportion of the farms — around 25 per cent of the arable land area — were forced into "cooperatives." In the "new," i.e., the ex-German, territories to the west there were also a substantial number of state farms. Although the collectives and the state farms were favored as to fertilizer and other supplies, and machinery and other capital goods, results were most unsatisfactory. Meanwhile on the remaining private farms there was a shortage of factors and resentment over the discriminatory taxation that was designed to force these producers into the collectives. So here production was stagnant, where it did not decline, and in any case deliveries fell as the peasants ate more of what they did produce.

Since October 1956 the situation has changed radically. Farmers were then told they might leave the collectives, and four fifths of those belonging departed forthwith. The discrimination in taxation, and especially in the supply of factors and funds to the private farmers, was dropped. Farm output has since been rising, and the new policy is regarded as at least one achievement of the Gomulka era that has proved itself.

The villages we visited yesterday had a thrifty look of well-being. The older houses were of heavy timber with a deep, beautiful thatch. The more recent ones were mostly of brick. The farmyards were tidy and full of healthy-looking livestock. The cows, mostly Holsteins, were of good quality, and the calves showed the advantages of artificial insemination. I had remembered Polish villages in the north as very untidy. These were not. However, I have little doubt that I was taken to see not the average but the best.

This morning I gave my first lecture. It was not a resounding success. The audience at the outset consisted mostly of faculty members. After I was well started a number of students came rushing in as though in answer to a riot call. I cannot persuade myself that the lecture was widely understood. I am glad that I did not have to listen to it in Polish.

After the lecture I fell into conversation with a

young teacher who took part in the Bor uprising
and who was seriously wounded fighting just outside the building where he now teaches. (The university is on the banks of the Vistula and was one
of the focal points of the conflict.) Although he is
anything but pro-Russian, he was not critical of the
Russians for failing to intervene. He thought they
recognized that the uprising was designed to antici-
pate them and was in degree directed against them.
Therefore, they had a right to keep their hands off.
By contrast, he was critical of what he characterized
as the romantic strategic concepts of the London
Poles who believed that such a seizure of power
would give them a position of strength against the
Russians. No government so completely astride the
Soviet lines of communication could have apprecia-
ble autonomy at this time. The effort involved a
needless loss of life. He thought the Czechs had been
wiser. "They postponed their revolt until the right
time: The only damage in Prague was to one mirror
and two glass doors."

Until October 1956 he had been forced to con-
ceal his participation in the uprising because of the
suspicion it incurred.

This afternoon I called at one of the ministries to
give the Minister a book and a letter of greetings

from Haberler.[1] They had been Rockefeller fellows
in the same year in the United States. The Minister
was obviously pleased and urged me to call back
again. I must avoid giving him the impression that
Haberler would be in accord with all aspects of Polish
economic policy.

Thereafter I cashed some cheques — Poland is
not inexpensive — and then went to look for a book-
store which is supposed to be exceptionally good.
It may be, but I could not find it.

Mostly I reflected on the drabness of life. One gets
the impression that people put on a very brave
front, but only as the result of infinite effort. I looked
into a toy shop which had the worst trinkets imagin-
able at very high prices. There was a long queue before what I took to be a dram shop, although I am
not sure. There are quite a few soldiers, mostly
officers, on the streets, but they are not very notice-
able, for many of the civilians wear a green-khaki
coat that has the appearance of a uniform. This may
be the problem of socialism. Planners can provide
for everything but color, and they cannot allow for
that because so much of it is associated with idiocy
great and small. In any case, the people of Poland
have more liberty than variety.

In the late afternoon I had a visit from a Polish

novelist. He was anxious to know how and by whom
I had been invited to Poland. Finally he blurted out:
"Surely you are not a Marxist, are you?" I told him
I wasn't but that I might be distinguished from some
non-Marxists by a realization that Poland had cer-
tain problems of location to live with. He nodded.

Tonight, by invitation of the ambassador but in
fact by arrangement of Harold Linder, I went to
an interesting dinner party at the British Embassy.
We had a long talk about events since 1956. The ambassador has good analytical sense and gave an able
interpretation of events. He thinks that in recent
months there has been a marked move in the direction of realignment with the Soviets. The discipline
of the bloc is being tightened and the Poles are
yielding. I asked him about an alternative hypothe-
sis, namely, that the Polish government is making
the right sounds on foreign policy while using its
autonomy to get ahead with needed changes on the
economic front. He thought this at least possible.

The ambassador pointed out that Poland was the
only eastern bloc country where all questions — including questions of party strategy — can be freely
discussed with members of the Communist Party.
This makes Poland the most interesting of all these
countries. While the ambassador is good, at least one

member of his staff is a primitive idiot. No American abroad is ever quite so bad as the British imperial strategist whose views are derived in equal parts from Kipling, Kitchener, and Cecil Rhodes. However, my Warsaw friend may have owed something to alcohol.

The Polish Economic Society

May 13

A very long day. This morning I went to the Yugoslav Embassy for my visa. The quarters are also being
built (or rebuilt). The officials had been duly advised
by Belgrade, and my visa was issued forthwith — although I was courteously relieved of a hundred zlotys
as a "taxe."

Then I went to the United States Embassy next
door and picked up some books. The marine guard,
clearly a lad of intelligence, was reading a copy of
American Capitalism. I told him he would go far,
even in the Marines. Then I went to visit the School
of Planning and Statistics. It is two or three kilometers from the center of Warsaw in one of the less
devastated parts of the city and is a large establish-
ment. (It dates from 1906 when, as the result of the
czarist concessions of that period, a school of economics, as it was then called, became possible.) Now
the students number some thousands. The buildings
— plain but light, airy, and more attractive than

31

most — are huge. Most are of postwar construction or reconstruction. An important part of the curriculum is the training of plant managers — "the Harvard Business School of Socialism," one professor observed. Economics, statistics, and foreign trade are among the other fields of specialization.

I visited the rector, a fine scholar of the old school — he recently succeeded Oskar Lange — and the pro-rector, and made the school a present of a half dozen books. They seemed much pleased. Then we had coffee and discussed the students — they are uninterested in politics, marry before they can properly support a wife, and have more time for studies now that they are on state scholarships. Foreign trade, because of its prospect for overseas travel, is the most popular field of study. Business management is not especially popular, although it pays slightly better than other fields. One of the professors remarked that the pressure for a doctrinaire egalitarianism is much stronger in Poland than in Russia. As a result, there is little difference in the rewards to different professions. The implication was that there should be more.

I toured the school and library in company of a succession of faculty members and ended up with a professor of business organization who, somewhat unpredictably, is also head of the school trade union. I asked him whom he bargained with on wages, and he replied, "Oh, all of that is centrally determined." I tried to get from him what the union did, but he was not very responsive. Faculty housing seems to be its main responsibility. I fear he is no John L. Lewis.

He is, however, a most delightful man, and after showing me some fine first editions in the library — of Hobbes among others — walked with me back to town. On the way we stopped at his apartment and had a vodka or two. He told me that only a Polish government which displays independence can have the support of the people. Given a choice between Germans and Russians, the first are the most to be feared. He says the fear of war is a phobia in Poland — "one thinks of it even in the movies" — and that Poland is the worst country in the world to govern because of its two hundred odd years of experience in resisting all government. He said he had difficulty understanding the difference between Democrats and Republicans, wanted to know if Stevenson would run again, and if I thought the case method [1] was scientific. To the last I said no, and he said he agreed.

I had had very little breakfast, and with all this I

had barely time to get to the Polish Economic Society for tea and my lecture. This lecture, which was on countervailing power,[2] went much better. The audience, which was assembled at the handsome quarters of the Society in downtown Warsaw, was mature and interested and followed me closely. Lange presided and was most courtly in his introduction and comments. Afterwards the questions lasted for an hour or more. These ranged from some fairly straight Marxian dissent to sympathetic queries as to details. One perceptive scholar asked why more Western economists did not accept so obviously sensible a resolution of the paradox of power instead of relying on competition. Lange brought me home, and I gave him my last copy of Dorfman, Samuelson, and Solow, which he wanted badly to see, and a carton of English cigarettes which I remembered his wife favored. Finally, at about 9:30, I got my first legitimate meal of the day. Ham and eggs only.

Notes on the way of life: A bus ride costs about three cents at the tourist rate. The streets are so clean that in the moonlight they shine. The workmanship on the buildings is very poor — the woodwork is of poor quality, the floors are badly laid, and the masonry is poorly joined.

The Polish Economic Society

During the war years the School of Economics, like all institutions of higher learning in Poland, was banned by the Germans. So it operated clandestinely as a secondary school. When the Germans inspected it, the teachers shifted to a permissible subject such as bookkeeping. The degrees then granted were later affirmed.

Academic Ceremony

May 14

Today was a holiday at the university while it cele-
brated its 150th anniversary. I attended by invitation
of the rector, and the ceremonies began with formal
introductions in the *Palais Jean Casimir,* the main
building of the university. A large number of foreign
visitors were on hand, and the array of academic
robes and gowns was brilliant. As a kind of unat-
tached visitor I was assigned a place in the academic
procession, along with a visiting Indian and one or
two others just behind the pro-rector of Peking, the
pro-rector of Hamburg, and (I believe) the representative of the University of Outer Mongolia. These
last were the youngest universities represented. The
procession was, of course, led by the University of
Paris. The representative of Outer Mongolia, if I
identified him correctly, had something of the academic aspect of Tony Galento. He seemed to be
worried about being photographed with me, so
whenever I approached he retreated. The only

American university officially represented was Columbia whose representative had been sent over from Munich. He obviously felt badly about not having academic attire or decoration — these had been specified in the invitation — so he had put his Phi Beta Kappa key in his buttonhole.

The procession wound slowly through the university grounds to the auditorium, with many pauses en route. Hearing me speak English, the Chinese representative appealed to me for some language assistance. He is a Chicago-trained physicist and sent his regards to various Harvard faculty members whom he met at the conferences sponsored by Cyrus Eaton at Pugwash, Nova Scotia.

The proceedings, being mostly in Polish, mostly escaped me. The rector, who evidently had something to say about academic freedom and traditions, was vigorously applauded. A professor of mathematics, he looked in his robes and ermine like an amiable but very intelligent Santa Claus. The Minister of Public Instruction, a politician of the general appearance and build of the late Paul Dever, was accorded perfunctory applause. I got from his speech only a reference to Marx and Lenin.

The crowd showed its preferences in an interesting way when the various representatives were called to present their credentials. The winners, by far, were Paris and Peking, although the latter owed something to his fine appearance and to the fact that he presented a great silk banner as his greeting. Columbia and Moscow came together and won about the same tactful reaction. The most conspicuous coolness was to the representative of the Karl Marx University of Leipzig.

The honorary degrees were distributed between East and West — Geneva, Oslo, Prague, etc. — and seemed to be nonpolitical so far as I could tell.

Eventually the proceedings palled, and during an intermission I slipped out. I had coffee with two women members of the faculty of economics, one of whom did her graduate work in Russia. She hopes soon to come to the United States. We discussed why wage and income differentials are narrower in Poland than in the U.S.S.R. She thought it because Poland has a more self-conscious and politically sensitive labor force. It is her view that the differential should be much wider. The Russian professorial salaries are well known in Poland — in some cases, for academicians in particular, they are nearly ten times as high as Polish salaries.

For meals this hotel serves only ham and eggs, and I lunched as usual on these staples. Then I was picked up by the Austrian minister with whom I had a long talk at his legation. He is exceedingly interest-

ing and well informed. However, much of our discussion was devoted to the general European situation. He thinks the Polish prospect is fairly satisfactory. His enthusiasm for American foreign policy
in general, and Dulles in particular, is restrained.

At six we went together to the *Palais Jean Casimir*
at the university to a reception given by the rector.
I saw a great many people that I knew — it is amaz-
ing how quickly one's acquaintance widens in a city
of this size. The rector of the University of Wroclaw
(Breslau) pressed me very strongly to visit him.
This was originally on my schedule but had to be
dropped for lack of time. Professor Schiller of Hamburg joined me, and later some Polish economists
from the university and planning board. I invited
them all to dinner at the Bristol, and the party continued until midnight. We ranged over the problems
of the United States, West German, and Polish economies. One of the Polish economists asked me how
I would run a country like Poland within a broadly
socialist framework. I replied that I would keep
agriculture private since both capitalist and socialist
experience showed the difficulty of applying socialism to this sector. (I hoped this might be considered
consistent with a "broadly socialist framework.") For
large enterprises I suggested that the critical question was managerial autonomy and not ownership.

39

The problem is to accord them the requisite independence of decision and in a context where the incentives favor socially desirable decisions. This does not exclude planning of investment aggregates — the amount to go to steel as compared with (say) cement.

Trade and small business, I suggested, should be the grounds for debate. However, I added that I had difficulty seeing the rationale for public ownership in this area. Few get rich; the market incentives obviously make people work hard. And if agriculture must be private, the acquisitive mentality, which will certainly exist in the case of trade, will not be unique.

My friend was much interested. He said he thought Poland was moving toward some such formula. He added, "Certainly if I am ever the adviser to a socialist America, I will not urge public ownership for handicrafts or small trade." But he concluded by saying — as everyone else does — that something must first be done to get price and wage relatives straightened out. If prices and costs are out of line autonomy, whether of small enterprises or large, leads to the wrong decisions.

I asked why the workers' state treated the peasants well and the workers less well — a fact often mentioned in conversation and clearly shown by the statistics. He replied that this was "Marxism accommodated to practical necessity." The peasants occupy the position of strategic power in a country heavily dependent on their willingness to produce efficiently.

A very interesting evening. Schnapps and dinner (without wine) for five was about six hundred zlotys, which is around twenty-four dollars at the tourist rate.

Technical note: The "accounting rate" of interest which is charged on investment now ranges from 7 to 10 per cent. The rate for savings is very low — 2 or 3 per cent. This, economists believe, should be much higher.

Stalinism in Poland is referred to as "the terrible past which may well lie before us."

Agricultural Institutes
and Colleges

May 15

This morning I went to the Institute of Agricultural Economics where I had a long talk with officials. The head, who was (I think) a Marxist, gave me a stronger defense of the past aims of postwar agricultural policy than any I have yet heard. However, it was far from being unqualified.

The coöperative or collectivization program, in his view, was not seen in its "organic setting." I gathered that this meant it was pressed too fast too soon. In the grain-producing areas it worked better than on the livestock or mixed farms. It was also a desirable and in some respects a necessary policy where the property in question had formerly been a single large estate and hence had but one set of buildings. It worked better in the progressive west than in the less advanced east. A choice as to the type of collective was given to the peasant — the range being from the holding of virtually all assets in common as in the U.S.S.R., to more limited types such as those providing for individual ownership of livestock but collective production of grain. (This latter allows consolidation of small plots and efficient use of power tillage and harvesting equipment.) The limited types worked better than the total collectives.

In the region of Poznan of about a thousand collectives, somewhere around a half still survive. These were either former large estates or enterprises which confined themselves to coöperative grain production. In the Breslau district, where the production was more mixed and the collectives more comprehensive, the number dropped from a thousand to seventy-five in October 1956. In eastern areas the number of collectives was always relatively small.

I asked if the experiment could be considered over. He said the next step would come much more slowly, for it would await acceptance of the peasants. It will indeed be slow in coming, I imagine.

He saw no great future for state farming. Most state farms, which are administered in groups of three to five, are in the new territories in the west. There is still a lack of enthusiasm for ownership or settlement in these areas. Elsewhere they are not likely to be of much importance.

There is a good deal of confusion in Polish agri-

43

cultural thinking, as the discussion this morning brought out. The importance of raising agricultural productivity is stressed. This would get the same output with fewer people. But there is also worry about the number of young people who are leaving the farms, and you hear it argued that peasant incomes must be good to keep people on the land. Yet everyone also agrees that Polish agriculture is overpopulated. These inconsistencies occasionally come into a single conversation.

This afternoon I strolled through the shopping area. It has suddenly become very warm and a large crowd was out. There was a long queue at a stand where lemons were for sale. In a food store there were two other long queues — one I think for freshly ground coffee, although I couldn't see without being obvious. I went into the largest department store which was far from prepossessing. I was impressed by the energy with which people dashed up the escalators until I saw that this was necessary for they were not running. The merchandise looks wretchedly poor.

At four I was picked up by a professor and taken on a tour of the college of agriculture and some state farms. The main part of the college is in a fairly distant suburb, and about a kilometer away our tubercular car (a Polish model which everyone criticizes) finally expired. We continued on foot and looked at the institution. Like so much else in Poland, one is put off by the awful shabbiness. I didn't really think it was very good, although one can't be sure. It is hard to judge a Department of Farm Management by looking at the offices and the charts on the wall.

Eventually our car was repaired and we visited two or three state farms — a couple of them with very large commercial orchards. I thought them generally workmanlike and efficient in appearance, but such conclusions are also of small value. You can get the same effect on a farm by spending more money than it earns. All were ex-seats of ex-Polish nobility.

My host told me that Polish prospects were poor — "We have to rebuild this country every twenty years, which is discouraging"; and that while agricultural efficiency was increasing, policies had been and were still exceedingly doctrinaire. Thus no satisfactory small tractor had been developed because, it was assumed, the machine and tractor stations would supply all the power and this could be in large units. Now, for the small farms, a small tractor is badly needed.

A terrific thunderstorm cut short our tour, and I returned to the hotel for dinner. My food habits are

45

becoming a trifle monotonous. Pending completion of the kitchen, the hotel serves only ham or eggs or both. I have had these whenever I have eaten here and, although excellent, the possible combinations are somewhat limited. The vodka is extremely helpful.

A further note: At the university celebrations Lange commented on the brilliance and variety of the academic dress in contrast with the University of Chicago. "You see the advantage of socialism when it has feudal traditions."

American Communists; Polish Prices

May 16

This morning I chatted with the people at the embassy and went for a long walk. For lunch, instead of ham and eggs, I had some vodka and a Pilsener beer. It was more interesting and seemed to be quite nutritious. Then I had a nice nap.

I lectured at six at the School of Planning and Statistics. On the way in to the lecture I fell into conversation with two men, one of my age and one older, who spoke English with a marked American accent. Both were American Communists who had been deported to Poland — one after forty years in the United States. They seemed very homesick — indeed, one said he was attending the lectures to hear an American voice. I felt sad; I do not contemplate with any pleasure a man who is serving a life sentence.

The lecture was well attended and uneventful.

Afterward I went to dinner at the journalists' club with a group of Polish economists. We talked about pricing problems. A new and "final" price reform is now under way which, it is hoped, will make it possible to accord increased control over production to the individual enterprise and to test performance by profits. Now, since in some plants costs are in excess of prices whatever the output, the best managers are those who make the biggest losses, for they produce the most. In the past, incentives have been based on output. The highest reward was to those who produced the most. But this leads to the waste of materials and labor, wrong product mixes, and other irrationalities. The new reform will be principally of producers' prices. It will not affect consumers' goods prices greatly. Instead, the rates of the turnover tax will be adjusted. However, this is merely the last of a series of such reforms. They take a long while to work out and tend to be obsolete by the time they are finished. One wonders, to coin a phrase, if the fault isn't with the system.

John Michael Montias, a Yale economist who has written on price-setting and other problems in the Polish economy, is very favorably regarded by the Polish economists.

I was asked if I had read the new book by Paul Baran[1] which is now being translated into Polish.

I confessed that I had not. It was suggested that Baran had written very astutely about the nature of capitalist development. I indicated that there might be some opportunity for discussion here.

A story: In Russia no one can speak his mind except Khrushchev. In Poland everyone can speak his mind except Gomulka.

There was passing mention of the new Russian Sputnik and more of the French crisis.

After dinner, at about eleven, I was picked up by the Gruson's driver and paid them a visit for an hour or two. I had an interesting chat with a Polish poet who told me that while the physical conditions of life are difficult the intellectual freedom is now quite satisfactory. Now it is far past bedtime, but thanks to my Churchill-type nap I am not very sleepy.

I needed something to read today and found a cheap edition of Frank Norris' *The Octopus*, product of a Leipzig publisher. The jacket says it is a valuable and vivid account of the grinding tendencies of American capitalism. I would think it a troublesome point for the average local reader that the grindees are ten-thousand-acre wheat ranchers. Kulaks. The jacket also explains, helpfully, that Norris' anarchistic tendencies are an "error."

Warsaw to Lublin

May 17

This morning early I packed one bag, met my escort from the Polish Economic Society, and journeyed across the Vistula to the East Station. There we took a train to Lublin. The train, consisting of two classes, was crowded almost to Indian standards. On board I was met by a second escort, another charming woman, from the Catholic University of Lublin. I was well managed.

The train made its way at a negligible rate across the countryside — much of it scrubby pine and poplar but some of it rather pleasant farm land. The villages are thatched and an occasional house is painted a powder blue — a sign, according to one of my guides, that it contains (or perhaps once contained) a marriageable daughter. Everywhere the apple and cherry trees were in blossom.

We got to Lublin about two and I was brought to the university in a bright red Skoda. The university is just across the street from the large party head-

quarters — "vis-à-vis" as one of my guides said with
a quick smile.

I was given a nice lunch by the father-rector —
vodka, special Polish canapés, pork chops, and red
wine. I also learned that the university still feels a
bit abused. Its social science faculty was closed in
1950, and permission has not yet been granted for
reopening it — although the effect, characteristically, is that the teaching continues under a different
name in a different department. In Poland the paro-
chial schools have been closed although religious,
meaning Catholic, instruction is now permitted in
the public schools. I noted that this went rather further than would be considered fitting in the United
States and, indeed, than in all candor I would ap-
prove. The resulting effort to differentiate the situation of Catholic Poland from that of the secular
United States did not prove useful. I got the subject
changed. My lecture was well attended, but I fear
that it had no great interest or meaning to anyone
except the presiding professor. The evolution and
modification of market competition cannot be of
much interest to people who have never thought
about competition before and never will again.

Dinner was at the flat — very modest but very
clean and civilized — of one of the professors. Several younger members of the faculty came in, and

the discussion turned on work abroad, the long time it took to get passports, and the poverty of the students and university. The university is supported by four special contributions each year in the churches plus the gifts of friends. It is the only Catholic institution of its kind in eastern Europe. Contributions from affluent American Catholics would not, I think, be unwelcome.

I came home early. We are housed in a fine, large, nineteenth-century hotel — a pleasant and spacious change after the compact modern rooms of the Grand Hotel in Warsaw. There was a slight *contretemps* when we discovered they had, logically enough, made up two beds in the bedroom — one for myself and one for my guide — and none in the large living room which I occupy. Things were straightened out.

The police patrol in pairs here with slung rifles. There is a soft drink in Poland called Agricola.

Tour of Lublin

May 18

Sunday morning in Lublin. Bright sunshine; wide, leafy streets; scrubbed children in Sunday best; breakfast of brown bread and coffee; outside the public radio playing songs from Gilbert & Sullivan.

Lublin is one of the oldest cities in Central Europe, and after breakfast we were taken on a superior tour by a distinguished local architect. We visited the old Dominican church, the cathedral, the old town with Italian-looking façades, and the quite picturesque (but quite modern) castle beyond the old walls. All interesting. All, incidentally, with plaques relating how many Poles were killed by the Germans in this spot or that or from this particular institution. (Our translator lost two brothers.) The recollection of Nazi slaughter is the one thing which unites everyone in this poor country.

After our city tour we visited some villages — less prosperous than those we saw earlier but neat and thrifty. On one farm the dog was eating his lunch out of the helmet of some long extinct German soldier. Then at two o'clock we went to lunch with the father-rector of the university. Also present, as a kind of co-host, was the rector of the Lublin State University.

The lunch, preceded by cherry-colored vodka, was excellent. Mostly we talked of the life and problems of the students, and after lunch the rector of the state university took me to see the student hostels of his institution. These buildings, like those of the university in general, are new and rather rough, and the ground around is yet unlandscaped. The students live six to a smallish room and sleep in double-deck beds. There are common rooms and clubrooms and at the head of the stairs an open space with busts or photographs of Marx, Engels, Lenin (the "patron saints" someone said in passing), and various Polish revolutionary and traditional heroes. In the girls' hostel I had a long discussion with six inhabitants of a room plus numerous visitors. I asked them what troubled them most (lack of hot water) and what most worried the management (lack of discipline and the extreme proximity of the male dormitory). They wanted to know how many students slept in a room at Harvard, when visiting hours were over, how much students were paid, and whether our students had a good canteen.

54

Then the rector — a professor of biology — took me to his flat to introduce me to his wife. She is some twenty-six years younger than he, half English, and a judge formerly of the local juvenile and now of the criminal court. I asked her about crime, which she says is more or less constant — about 90 per cent being theft. Alcoholism is a grave complicating factor which she described as a most serious problem in Polish social life. She also observed that it would not be remedied until other goods become abundant and inexpensive. Now a man cannot buy his family a decent living, so he does what he can which is to get blind. Alcoholism among children is, she says, a growing and especially sad problem. Parents teach their eight- and ten-year-olds to drown their youthful troubles.

I told her that if ever I took up a criminal career I would hope to patronize her court. She replied that she would be delighted to have me as a customer.

Back at the Catholic University there was a cocktail party — Yugoslavian wine to be exact — followed by a visit to the library. Yet to come this evening is a late dinner after which I take the sleeper to Cracow. I am already very weary.

Cracow

May 19

I had dinner last night with an architect in Lublin —
it was pleasant and almost sumptuous, and his flat
(which he shared with two other families) was a
museum of Polish ceramics and art and of old books
— mostly French first editions on art and philos-
ophy. He showed them with much pride.

The train from Lublin to Cracow — another grad-
ual conveyance — was crowded but we had clean
and pleasant berths in a prewar Wagon-Lits. I slept
fitfully, but this was partly because I had dined too
well. We got to Cracow at about 7:30 this morning.

We were met and breakfasted by members of the
Cracow branch of the Polish Economic Society and
housed in a pleasant nineteenth-century hotel — also
spacious in comparison with Warsaw modern. The
maid, a slender, aristocratic-looking lady in her
fifties or early sixties, spoke clear, precise English.
Then we went on a tour of Cracow, guided by a

professor of art and architecture — the Marien-
kirche with fine stained glass and its magnificent
carved altarpiece, Wawel Palace, the Cathedral, the
old university, the market places. Cracow was un-
damaged by the war — the Germans had to evacu-
ate quickly to avoid being cut off — and it is truly
one of the most beautiful cities in Europe.

After paying respects to the rector — a professor
of the history of art — we lunched at the journalists'
club. At five I gave the first of three lectures. The
audience followed me closely, and the questions
were friendly and good. Unlike the Warsaw lectures,
there was a fairly complete summary in Polish.

I had planned to give but one lecture. However,
three had been scheduled and I agreed to the
change. Everyone was pleased when I said that I
was being exploited by the workers' state. This re-
minds me of the most popular Polish story. Do
you know the difference between capitalism and
communism? Under capitalism man exploits man.
Under communism it is just the reverse.

After the lecture I had an odd accident. With one
or two of the professors I strolled through the streets
and parks — the latter are rich and green and burst-
ing with lilacs — and eventually I turned off close
to my hotel. Then I discovered that I was not on the
right street and also that on my arrival this morning

I had not noticed the name of my hotel. After some search I made my problem known — or tried to — in another hotel. The clerk took me to be a candidate for the local insane asylum. My having failed to notice either the name of the hotel or that of the street seemed to him wholly implausible. The conversation was in German and I was conscious that I was making no sense. But presently he directed me to another hotel where I would at least be understood. This turned out to be mine.

With the curious exception of the *Daily Express*, which I encountered the other day, I have just seen the first English paper since my arrival. It is the *Daily Worker*, and I suppose one should be thankful for small blessings.

It is said here that during the Hungarian revolt everyone behaved like someone else. The Russians behaved like Germans. The Hungarians behaved like Poles. The Poles behaved like Czechs. The Czechs behaved like swine.

Samuelson's *Principles*[1] is to be translated here. They are waiting for the last edition.

Last night in Lublin I investigated the position of lawyers in the socialist state. A few practice privately. The rest are joined in collectives, and fees are charged for the group as a whole and divided with due regard to rank. The principle may come from Sullivan and Cromwell.

I learn that I was the object of quite a tug-of-war in Lublin between the Catholic and the state university. My visit to the hostels of the state university and to the rector's flat helped keep things in balance.

Everywhere I hear grateful comments on books received from CARE and the embassy.

Overcrowding in Cracow is as serious as in Warsaw. The city has doubled in population since the late thirties, and there has been little building. The churches are also overcrowded, even on a weekday or weekday evening. However, May and June are holy months.

Steel and the City Hall

May 20

At nine I was taken to Nowa Huta, some ten kilometers from Cracow, to see the new town and the vast new steel complex. About a hundred thousand live in the town, all of which is new in the last eight years. It is rather stark but also rather impressive. The steel works — *Huta im Lenina* officially, although ordinary reference is to Nowa Huta — is immediately adjacent and covers an area of some three or four square miles. A young English-speaking engineer took us over the plant which, to my rather unpracticed eye, was impressive and fairly workmanlike. By our standards, however, it gives the unmistakable impression of being undermaintained, especially as to paint and polish, and it could certainly do with a larger clean-up and sweeping gang. One of my companions drew my attention to a decaying sign urging completion of the Six Year Plan as a matter of "honor" and noted that such propaganda was now confined to the safety drive. I asked him if it had lost its effect on the workers and he replied, "No, it never had any." Some suggest, however, that at an earlier stage Polish workers showed a good deal of enthusiasm.

The plant is obviously a source of considerable pride. One engaging feature is that the space between the endless ranks of buildings, tracks, and stacks is heavily planted with trees. The effect is to make it look a little like a steel plant in a newly-planted park.

On the way back to Cracow we visited a couple of interesting old churches, and then I was taken to see the rector of the School of Economics. He asked me about class distinction in the United States. I told him that I thought wealth was becoming less a source of prestige and that intellectual achievement and politics were probably becoming more important. He asked me about the position of scientists. I told him that while the Sputniks had been helpful one should not suppose that scientists had previously been precisely a depressed caste.

Next I was received by the mayor at the city hall. He is a professor of economics and promptly queried me about my books. (I discover that a local literary review has just dealt with them, and hence everyone is well briefed.) I then signed the visitors' register which has been kept continuously since the thirteenth century. My inscription — "May your revenues always exceed every conceivable need" — attracted general approval.

I asked the mayor what were his most important problems. He said they were housing, schools, and the deficit in municipal transport. Not new.

I tried, not too successfully, to get a picture of revenue sources. These include municipal utilities and would include rents except that these are abnormally low and return little over cost. So the state has assigned some industrial enterprises to city management under the decentralization plan. I gather these are now expected to make an important contribution. None of this should be regarded as definitive.

My lecture, at five, was in the impressive Senate Room of the university — under the portraits of the past rectors in their official garb. The summary in Polish and questions took until eight at which time I was taken to dinner by the professors. Conversation turned on the Germans and the occupation period — an endlessly recurring theme — and the treatment of the university. All professors had been called to a lecture on the attitude of the German occupation to science. Once assembled, all were arrested and taken to Sachsenhausen or Oranienburg. Release came only after a number had died and on intervention of the Italian government and the Holy See.

My next neighbor, an American-trained professor, lost his job in 1950 and was rehabilitated last year. I asked why he had been dismissed, and he said he didn't know — "Of course I'm not a Marxist." I formed the impression that one of his derelictions could have been extreme dullness.

I got back to the hotel toward eleven, very tired and with a splitting headache. Tomorrow I have another lecture and a trip to Warsaw, but first we go (starting at six) to see villages in the Carpathians.

To the Mountains and Warsaw

May 21

We left at six this morning for a trip to Zakopane in the Carpathians, about a hundred kilometers from Cracow. The drive was most pleasant. The rolling country is in contrast with the flat plains around Warsaw, and the hills were spotted with apple orchards in full blossom. The peasants were everywhere busy with their spring seeding. The mountains, when we reached them, were agreeable but unspectacular. Zakopane is a resort town somewhat resembling a Swiss ski center, and we had breakfast at a milk bar that was overrun by young hikers. I found a good picture or two of houses and costumes.

By twelve we were back in Cracow for my third and final lecture. Then after a late lunch we went to the station — the usual crowds — and with the agile help of my professor escort I got a seat. The station and platform were incredibly hot and so was the train. I was badly dressed for it in a heavy tweed sport jacket. I have rarely been more uncomfortable.

However, the train was fast and fairly modern, and I got some supper in the restaurant car. This is something of a gamble when you do not know the language and cannot even guess. But I hit upon the *table d' hôte* and did very well.

On the car, as in restaurants generally, the food was heavy, with great emphasis on potatoes, but well cooked and agreeable. It is served with approximately the elegance of a Canadian threshing bee. Dinner plus a bottle of beer (warm but useful) cost about Z40 or $1.60 at the tourist rate. I was back in Warsaw at ten where I was met and brought back to the Grand Hotel ORBIS.

In the Cracow station is a large mural of how Nowa Huta is to look when finished. It is very brilliant and grand. The reality is a good deal less.

A well-informed individual has given me an account of the economic policy of the early fifties. Investment goods naturally had a high priority in the Six Year Plan, and in 1951 and 1952 the tensions accompanying the Korean War brought a great increase in armament investment. Adjusting for the relatively low level of capital goods prices, he thinks that with defense Poland was investing about 40 per cent of national income in 1952. This brought a reduction in living standards and, along with the collectivization, cultivated the discontent which culminated in the 1956 disorders. Now arms investment has been much reduced, but there is still a deep conviction that this generation must sacrifice for the next — "We face twenty years of austerity." I asked him why this generation should give up so much for the next — why, since it isn't a question of starvation or physical privation, people now living might not be given a better break at the price of a slower rate of growth. He said there was an increasing tendency to make this argument.

On the railroad from Cracow one passes two large enclosures with watch towers and surrounding fences — in one case with elaborate lights. Inside are industrial plants and also barracks. The guard towers now seem abandoned, and the gates of one enclosure were open.

On the train I saw the only Russian soldiers since I have been here — apart from the officers whom one encounters at the hotel. There seems to be a fairly steady flow of high officers through the hotel.

Last Day in Warsaw

May 22

My last lecture was at ten at the university. The attendance was good and the discussion, which was alert and friendly, lasted until about noon. Then, with a charming woman economist from the university, I called on Lange at the Parliament. The Chamber was in session, and we listened to a speech or two while Lange — who sits on the ministerial bench — was being told of our arrival. About half the seats were filled. In reassuring parallel with Western democracy no one was paying the slightest attention. The position here is an interesting one and not well understood. In the democratic state the representative requirements of government take far more people than can, in fact, be employed in the business of governing. To avoid the disaster of their participation, but while also avoiding the appearance of idleness, we have speeches. Any number of people can be occupied in making speeches or, more particularly, in serving as an audience. While it is often supposed that speeches are for the purpose of communicating ideas, in fact they are primarily for the purpose of disguising the unemployment that is inevitable in the democratic process. I was glad to see that this great democratic invention is also useful in a Communist state.

Lange and I chatted for half an hour and then I went on to an embassy luncheon. It was an interesting group including a correspondent for the party paper, a professor of economics, and the head of the foreign section of the trade unions — an erstwhile American union organizer and Communist party member who returned some years ago to Poland. There were also a number of Americans from the embassy staff. Polish economic problems were discussed at length. The Polish party people were very critical of the management of plants and enterprises, but I did not pick up much that was new.

After lunch I visited the Polish Economic Society and inscribed copies of various books to people — Leontief [1] to the newly-elected dean of the Faculty of Economics, Duesenberry[2] to the secretary of the Polish Economic Society, and lesser works to lesser men. (To Mrs. Massalska of the Society, who has been my friend, counselor, and guide, I gave a compact. In spite of herself I think she preferred it to a book.)

At five I was to be interviewed by the overseas English service of the Polish radio. But after some reflection I declined. The questions, which they had given me in advance, were quite innocent. But any overseas radio operation is for propaganda purposes. I suspect that scholarly goals are best served by avoiding even the appearance of such involvement. I wouldn't advise a Polish professor who is in the United States to go on the Voice of America. I did give a press interview which was briefly reported.

During the afternoon I had a long talk with another former American Communist Party member who was either deported to Poland some years ago or who left in anticipation of immediate deportation. He has seen a lot of Polish workers and is an old and experienced party worker and organizer. He says the workers are in a difficult mood. If asked, they would say, with all sincerity, that they are against a return to capitalism. But they are equally against the present order. The great mistake, he believes, was in the promises that were made during the Six Year Plan. These were taken seriously, and at first the workers responded. But when the better life did not materialize they were disappointed and disillusioned. He criticized the government for talking of its machines, which are vastly inferior to those of American factories. Where it has a point — welfare and paid college education for workers' families — it is silent.

I asked him what the workers wanted. He said, "I don't really know — just a better life. They want a system that works. They don't know what that is."

Finally, I asked him how he found his own life in Poland. He said, "The work is interesting enough. But if you want the truth, I'm homesick as hell." I would gather he thinks socialism still might work, but not in Poland.

He told me his wife and child have just got a visa to visit the United States. Now he has to struggle to get a Polish exit permit for them while the United States visa is still valid. He made an interesting conversational slip. "My wife was never a Communist. She is completely honest."

Tonight a final dinner from the Polish Economic Society. It was in a restaurant in the Old Town in the celler of a building that once belonged to Jakob Fugger the Rich. (The last of the Fuggers, eighty and without issue, is a wine-taster for the government.) The dinner was most cordial and even merry. I had a long talk with Lange. He thinks the long-run problems between Communist and non-Communist countries will far more involve China than Russia. He says the sense of resentment in China over exclusion from the U. N., over Formosa, and the con-

tinued quasi-isolation is very great. We also talked
of Polish economic matters but covered ground already discussed. Many affirm the anomaly of the
way the workers' state discriminates, relatively at
least, against the workers. Since Poland has a highly
intelligent working force, as well as a highly developed intelligentsia, these are the politically decisive groups in the community. The poor deal
accorded these groups does seem to me politically
incomprehensible. The price elasticity of supply of
agricultural products is high; i.e., there is a favorable
response to good farm prices. So it is good business
to treat the peasants well. But, this being so, the only
course is to stretch out the industrialization period
— let this generation have some of the gains, rather
than reserve them for the next. But here one encounters the Calvinist conviction that there must
be rapid growth to a high future goal which means
sacrifice now. These sacrifices are not, incidentally,
for military purposes. Everyone seems to agree that
Poland does not now need to make large military in-
vestments. However, judging only from the soldiers
one sees, the military budget must still be considerable.

Note on the lesser evil: at lunch the slow mails
came up for discussion. (It often takes a week for
a foreign letter to clear the Warsaw Post Office.)

The university professor said, "The reason is simple. It's the censorship." A correspondent for the party paper and one or two other officials argued that there was none. They claimed it was only inefficiency.

My American Communist friend asked me what I thought of Nowa Huta which he had visited. I told him I thought it looked fairly workmanlike but dirty. He said that in the past it had been ridiculously overstaffed but that this had been remedied. As to the plant housekeeping, he agreed it was terrible. "In the United States I would say to management, 'Clean up this place or I pull out the men.' "

At dinner one economist, another agreeing, made an impressive point. He said, "We have argued against our more orthodox colleagues that there can be sustained growth under capitalism. Now with the recession we already hear it said that we were wrong. Do you realize what a test this is for your economy — and for our reputations?"

A note from yesterday: While coming down from the mountains the car radio was playing a Russian song. My companion said, "It is almost a welcome change. Until two years ago we heard nothing else. Now we have only American and French jazz."

Warsaw to Belgrade

May 23

At a little after eight this morning I was taken to the airport by two of my economist hosts, and after various formalities took off on the Polish airline LOT for Belgrade. The plane stops en route at Budapest and proceeds to Tirana from Belgrade if there are passengers for or at the latter outpost. (The hostess hopes there won't be.) The plane is a Soviet type, somewhat resembling a small Convair, and as I write it is flying adequately. At the exchange control I had to show my money and was sent back to spend a hundred zlotys that I still had and could not bring out. The only purchasable commodity was chocolate with which I am now adequately supplied. Two young women on the plane are better tailored and groomed than anyone I have seen in Poland — and attract attention by the fact. I have discovered that they are Hungarian and bound for Budapest.

One or two further observations on Poland. Only once was there a suggestion of secret police activity.

73

A foreign diplomat with whom I talked (not United States) said his house was not safe and he kept the radio going while we conversed. Nothing that he said seemed very dangerous by Polish standards, and it is my over-all impression that the police, if they do listen, must be astonished when they hear anything that isn't critical of the government.

More generally, the problem of Poland seems to be one of reconciling a very high state of intellectual achievement with a very low level of economic life. Everyone is aware that life is better in Western Europe, and this is the standard for comparison. The result is deep dissatisfaction and articulate and un-inhibited criticism. A narrow and restrained economic life is no doubt possible in a culturally backward community, and many such communities would think Polish standards highly satisfactory. But such contentment cannot so easily coexist with a brilliantly critical intellectual life.

A further point must be emphasized. Geography makes a socialist economic order more or less an imperative. Even the least reconciled do not talk of much change here. While good relations with the U.S.S.R. are essential, even the most ardent Communists with whom I talked consider themselves Poles first. This is a point of major importance for the United States. Certainly the notion that all Communists take their orders willingly and automatically from Moscow — Tito of course excepted — can be a prime source of error.

Finally. It is hard to overestimate the desire of the Polish intellectuals, again including a good many members of the high bureaucracy and press — and in particular the university people — to be considered part of the West. In the universities, incidentally, it is difficult to exaggerate the role that the Ford Foundation is playing as a window to the West. Literally everyone you encounter is dreaming of a visit to Western Europe or the United States. Without this prospect one imagines that life for quite a few, especially of the younger people, would seem hopelessly dull and uninviting. A "Ford Fellowship" is the new Jerusalem.

My lectures are to be published as a book in Poland and both translation and publication have been arranged. Many apologies have been made for the inability to transmit royalties, but they are to accumulate to my account in zlotys. So I shall have a certain capital position come the revolution.

Later

We arrived in Belgrade about noon. We taxied up to the ramp by a museum of ancient plans including a Fokker tri-motor. I was welcomed by a cordial dele-

75

gation headed by Dr. Stanovnik,[1] and we drank Turkish coffee while formalities were being completed by proxy. Then we drove into Belgrade where I am most pleasantly housed in a small hotel overlooking the erstwhile palace and its adjacent park. Dr. Stanovnik and I had lunch and a long talk. His great concern is to develop a kind of pragmatic Marxism — to rationalize socialist economic ideas by stripping off the influence of irrelevant or obsolete ideology and incorporating what is relevant and important from more modern economic work.

After a nap I walked for an hour or two through the main shopping streets. The contrast with Warsaw could scarcely be more striking. The stores are filled with goods and, partly since there are more imports, they seem to be of far better quality. There is more traffic and the people lack the drab, uniform appearance of Poland. It is immediately evident that this is a far less egalitarian society. This latter is an important point.

Visitors regularly attribute to wealth what they should attribute to its distribution. One forms his impressions of the well-being of a community from the number of automobiles on the streets, the number of well-dressed women on the sidewalks, the elegance of the shops, and the number of fine houses or apartment buildings. But only a small minority needs to be well off to suggest such opulence. A community with a higher but more nearly equal distribution of income can have fewer such amenities or luxuries and thus give the impression of less wealth and well-being.

But to return to Belgrade. The difference from Warsaw is also in the cafes, the chestnut trees along the streets, and above all in the varied, pleasant buildings of what is at least a slightly older European city. These are wonderfully more agreeable than the stark social realism of Poland. And even the modern buildings of which there are many in the parts of the city that were damaged, are softer and less severe than in Poland.

One disappointment. I was to have had a session with Tito, but it has been cancelled. The explanation was candid. There are other Americans coming to town whom he cannot see. He could not see me without seeming to discriminate in my favor. From the context I imagine my competitors are politicians.

At dinner time there was a severe storm, and while making my way into the hotel restaurant I met a tall, handsome, and (by the standards of this part of the world) very well-dressed woman in her late twenties. She seemed to be sheltering from the rain. She smiled and asked me how long I had been in Belgrade. I told her and invited her to have a drink with me. This led on to dinner.

She makes her living being agreeable to visitors, more especially those in the smaller and "more discreet" hotels. She lives with her parents, both office workers, but has a small apartment for more relaxed moments. The work is not demanding, and she attributed her good looks to the fact that she gets a lot of rest. She says she meets an interesting class of people of whom, on the whole, she finds the Germans best combine affectionate and gentlemanly manners with requisite intellect. Americans she somewhat unpredictably described as "much like Englishmen." Her greatest problem is the high cost of clothes, and she listed some prices which did sound rather stiff. Her apartment is also not very satisfactory — not sufficiently private — and this is difficult to remedy in so overcrowded a city. Her line of work may not enjoy a particularly high priority.

After dinner I strolled with my informant to her apartment but then discontinued my research with a small gift. In the course of conversation she had mentioned the unfortunate ubiquitousness of police surveillance in "these Communist countries," and this, along with the novelty of my surroundings, acted as a reinforcement to normal virtue.

Drive into Serbia

May 24

A most interesting day. This morning I strolled around Belgrade looking for pictures and found a few interesting people and street scenes. Then at ten I called by appointment on the undersecretary of the Planning Board. We had a long and informative talk punctuated by schnapps and coffee. He thinks the Yugoslavs have succeeded in breaking through the crust of backwardness and getting the industry that is necessary for sustained growth. The worst problems are the continuing imbalance in the external position — the large balance of payments deficit — and the tendency (as in Poland) for more gains to accrue to peasants than to workers. We talked about time preferences in planning — how much should be sacrificed in the present for a higher living standard in the distant future. The Yugoslavs are not so Calvinist as the Poles. They are committed to supplying consumers' goods, including those that must be imported, in the present. This is in line with a pronouncement of Tito who has said that those who won socialism should enjoy at least some of its fruits. The great current argument is over how much reliance should be placed on foreign aid and foreign assistance. Should this be taken while the taking is good? Shouldn't every opportunity be seized to raise living standards as well as investment? But isn't dependence on such foreign aid dangerous? Wouldn't economic independence at a lower level of consumption and investment be wiser in order to protect political independence?

Some of these matters were also discussed later at an informal session at Dr. Stanovnik's Institute. The discussion was very gay and easy-going. About a dozen staff members participated. Then after lunch I was taken for a drive deep into the heart of Serbia to the south of Belgrade. This is a gently and then more steeply rolling country yielding eventually to mountains. The farms are small and primitive but look productive as do the vineyards. We visited the tombs of the kings of Serbia and Yugoslavia, most of whom seem to have been immigrants.

Also we passed the place where eighty thousand Yugoslavs, including Jews, were shot by the Germans during the war. A town nearby still forbids Germans, East or West, to remain overnight.

My companion, a young intellectual from the Institute, told me the following:

(1) The police are no longer a factor in one's life.

(2) On the whole, intellectuals feel tolerably well satisfied with their situation and freedom.

(3) The favorite American novelists are Hemingway and Faulkner, and among playwrights Arthur Miller and Tennessee Williams.

I saw Tito today. He was proceeding at a high speed in a four-car convoy when we met him. A motorcyle outrider moved us off the road and to a stop while he passed. It occurs to me that men in power, if they are wise, will always travel at a moderate rate of speed and preferably in modest cars. Nothing can possibly create a worse impression than big black limousines tearing through the countryside and forcing the common people to jump for their lives.

I was taken to dinner in a delightful outdoor restaurant on a hill near Belgrade. After the austerity of Poland I still find myself reveling in the luxury of life here — excellent food and wine, good service, and people who seem to be enjoying themselves. I suspect that I am too much of a hedonist to make a good modern socialist. The same might be true of the Yugoslavs.

81

Agricultural Tour

May 25

We went today to look at farms and villages to the north of Belgrade. It was a beautiful sunny summer Sunday, and youth day, and Marshal Tito's birthday to boot. Everyone was outdoors and even the peasant women looked well dressed and handsome. Youngsters were everywhere in jerseys and shorts, the girls making a point of extreme abbreviation. On the several roads into Belgrade a relay race was in progress. The winning baton was to be delivered to the Marshal.

We drove in a Pobeda north to Novi Sad and then on nearly to the Hungarian border. This country, the Danubian plain, is level, rich, and pleasant but far from exciting. The villages, where the peasants live, are exceedingly large — sometimes as many as ten thousand people — and in between are correspondingly great stretches of open land without houses. The farmers travel great distances to their land.

I had hoped to wander through villages and old towns, and take pictures, and I had made my wishes tolerably clear. But the socialist inevitable happened — I was taken to an experiment station, a hybrid corn breeding station, an irrigation experimental farm, and a state farm. These are the only presentable culture. Incidentally, the experiment stations seemed very good — far better equipped, more workmanlike, and more self-confident than those I saw in Poland.

At midmorning we had schnapps and vermouth and at noon in Novi Sad a notable meal with more alcohol. Then we had wine and soda during the afternoon. I consumed lightly, having regard to the hot weather and the danger of extreme drowsiness. One of my hosts asked if we were unaccustomed to drinking in the United States.

One of my guides had been an exchange student in plant genetics at the University of Illinois. Competent, self-assured, and determined to raise the level of his science in Yugoslavia, he was a monument to the virtues of this enterprise.

I arrived back in Belgrade very late for a party given by one of the cultural attachés at the embassy. It was a nice homelike party with well-groomed, slim, and attractive young wives getting systematically stewed.

83

There is some excitement over a birthday greeting from Khrushchev to Tito implying he isn't a fascist beast. He wasn't — he was — all was forgiven — he had just become one again — and now this telegram for what it may mean. Such incredibly foolish behavior. I am tempted to think, on the basis of my tour, that Poland and Yugoslavia are unique in Europe for the absence of anti-Americanism. For this, the Russians are to be thanked. One of my guides today was a former Partisan and, I imagine, an old Communist. When I happened to say, anent something or other, that the Russians had fought hard in World War II, he promptly jumped on me. What about that pact with the Germans before the war? Anyway, look how they were defeated at the beginning. They couldn't organize a front until they got British and American supplies." When I expressed doubt on the latter point, he was adamant although he conceded that Russian manpower losses had been high. Then he reminded me again of the Molotov-Ribbentrop pact. But he concluded the argument by saying generously, "Of course, I admit that you should do something about Dulles."

As we passed an airfield outside of Belgrade in the morning, our attention was drawn to masses of red poppies which stretched in a solid carpet seemingly to the horizon. I pointed out that these flowers supported the regime. One of my companions responded without a moment's hesitation, "But it is not required. A hundred flowers can bloom."

A current Yugoslav identification of the difference between capitalism and socialism: "Capitalism makes social mistakes, and socialism makes capital mistakes."

Lecture

May 26

At last an easy day, my first since I arrived in Poland. I got up late, worked on my lectures, and later went for a stroll. I am still impressed by the air of well-being and by the number of good-looking and well-groomed women. At twelve I gave my first lecture. It was not translated, but all attending were given a full text in Serbo-Croat. The room was packed; there was a good number of high officials, also a sizable delegation from the embassy. By arrangement there was no discussion of this lecture, it being purely historical, although I was challenged in a friendly way for citing Joan Robinson on Marx's view of Say's Law.

I lunched with some of the economic staff of the embassy. They are well impressed by the Yugoslav economy, as am I on brief observation.

In the evening I went to a reception at the ambassador's residence — small and pleasant — and then on to dinner with two high Yugoslav economic officials. Both are old Partisans and both had had a period of postwar service in Washington. The result, which I believe to be typical, was that they had developed a deep interest in American politics and folkways. Both are strong Yugoslav nationalists but also more than half American in outlook and interests. Nothing in this part of the world strikes one with more force than the existence of pro-American Communists.

We discussed agricultural matters and the danger of leaving agricultural policy to the technical agriculturalists. These have a great strategic advantage in policy making, for the average urban-minded official is likely to be either very insecure in his knowledge of agriculture or unaware of his ignorance. The technical agriculturist, on the other hand, is likely to have poor quantitative sense and often disperses rather than concentrates his efforts. We also discussed the time discount system of the socialist state. They affirmed the Yugoslav view that life should be enjoyed in the present. In their view the cause of socialism has been deeply damaged by those who call for severe sacrifices indefinitely continued. People are not impressed by the prospect of affluence in the indefinitely distant future.

We dined on an outdoor terrace at the Metropole, a vast, newly-completed hotel of most luxurious aspect. No workers' barracks this.

Informal Seminar

May 27

My second lecture was uneventful with a good attendance. The American ambassador attended, although I am not sure he found the subject fascinating.

In the afternoon I met for two or three hours with fifteen or twenty professors and assorted intellectuals at the apartment — most pleasant — of one of my hosts, and during the course of the seminar we were well fed and wined. The discussion centered on the influences and pressures which bear upon the modern capitalist state — and particularly on the government of the United States. No one seemed to question that these are far more complex than in the traditional Marxist system. The meaning of these ideas, as they bear on the willingness of the state to intervene in recessions, was discussed. I was asked if I thought the Eisenhower administration was using the current recession to destroy or gravely weaken the unions. I expressed doubts. I warned against at-

88

tributing to any of our politicians too elaborate or intricate a strategy — in particular, any strategy that the strategists themselves could not wholly grasp or agree on. It was a very interesting and highly undogmatic discussion.

The Yugoslavs, in their concern for inquiring what is to be retained from Marx and what is to be rejected, engage in a great deal more theoretical discussion than one encounters in Warsaw. Preoccupation in Warsaw is far more with practical problems. It could also be that Marx is taken less seriously in Poland, so there is less concern with revision. However, I am obviously generalizing here from limited data.

In the evening I had dinner with two United States girls who are wandering through Yugoslavia and afterward took them to have coffee and strawberries at the Metropole. Their efforts to understand the Yugoslav economy, if not successful, were at least praiseworthy. We were joined during the evening by one of the Garsts of Coon Rapids, Iowa. He is busy selling hybrid corn to the satellites.

Incidentally, when the Metropole was mentioned in conversation yesterday, someone said, "Ah, yes! We believe it to be the largest whore house under socialist management in the world."

More on Agriculture

May 28

My third lecture today went about as usual. A number of high government and party people were on hand, and there is to be a general discussion following my final lecture tomorrow. I lost the United States Ambassador but picked up the Canadian.

The head of the U.S.I.S. mission gave me a luncheon which included two or three leading Yugoslav economists — Marxists, and one a leading party theorist. We discussed the relevance of modern western economic theory to the problems of economic planning. They suggested that neo-Keynesian models were the most important macroeconomic guide and that the Leontief [1] input-output system, given the aggregate system, was especially important as a planning model. One suggested that Leontief was more important for a socialist than a capitalist economy and added an amusing observation: "You might bear in mind that if the Soviets had behaved wisely, Leontief would have grown up

90

in Russia. His work would then have been done in its logical context."

We had a long discussion about what American books should be translated, an enterprise which U.S.I.S. assists. The Yugoslavs held out for the best theoretical and technical books even though the circulation would be small. "Otherwise, some of our best people, who do not read English, will read only the Marxian literature. They don't necessarily wish to be dogmatic. They have no opportunity to be otherwise." Some of the U.S.I.S. people argued for books of more general interest and appeal. I said I thought the Yugoslavs had a point. Anyhow, the next one on the list is not at issue; again it is Samuelsons' *Principles*.

Later, I called by appointment on the chief agricultural planner at the Planning Ministry. We talked about agriculture for an hour, although through an interpreter. The period of the Russian blockade stopped all investment in agriculture, and there followed several years of near stagnation. For the last two or three years, however, output has been rising steadily. The trend will continue upward, and they are counting on their increased outlays in the new Plan period for fertilizer, hybrid corn, and machinery. (I am not persuaded that they are investing enough in fertilizer which, after all, is a substitute for land. This is an example of the failure of the technical agriculturist to identify the first essentials and concentrate on them.) The policy of forced collectivization is, of course, over. Emphasis henceforth will be on voluntary coöperation including pooled use of arable land and machinery where the peasants are willing. "But we are prepared to take time. We want a free agriculture." I get the impression that these latter changes are not expected to amount to much for a very long time.

A stubborn problem in Yugoslav agriculture is that of regional differences in income. While the ceiling on the permissible land holding — at the most about fifteen arable acres with an average of ten — holds for the whole Republic, some farmers make far more from this area than others. In Slovenia, net income per farm is four to five times what it is in Macedonia. (Later I saw some figures which seemed to throw doubt on this.)

I had dinner with some American embassy friends including a former Littauer student. They are old Yugoslav hands and well impressed by the economic progress, especially of the past three years. In their view, Yugoslavia now has a workable and a reasonably effective economy with a high growth. We discussed Russian policy toward Yugoslavia and the satellites, and the phenomenon of the pro-American

Communists. After all, if a Communist is a national-
ist, he is in trouble with Russia. So he identifies himself elsewhere, and that means with the United
States, and if he has been in the United States he
usually likes it. My friends are no longer surprised
by this. I even find myself getting accustomed to it.

A General View
of the Economy

May 29
My last lecture today with an hour's discussion following. I am glad they are over although I think,
on the whole, they were fairly successful. Someone
has noted that they were the first such full-dress ex-
position by a bourgeois economist in a Communist
country since the Russian revolution. I find this
nourishing to my vanity. A director of one of the
other economic institutes, in a speech of thanks, said
"Certainly what we have heard in these lectures is
not what we used to read in the books." (I was later
asked if there might be a further and final discussion
of the lectures tomorrow at noon.)

This afternoon I called by appointment on the
editor of the leading economic journal and an important party theoretician. He thinks Yugoslav economists are going in too much for econometrics and
formal and irrelevant theory. He said he gathered

94

that there were similar tendencies in the United States. I told him that, since it was possible that we had even more economists than economic problems, something needed to be done to keep our profession employed. He said the Yugoslav situation was less luxurious.

He thinks the economy is in good shape and will continue to expand at a satisfactory rate. The problem again is to keep the terms of trade from turning too much in favor of the peasants. In Yugoslavia, as in Poland, the peasants rather than the workers have, to date, been the principal beneficiaries of the worker's state. (The party, someone else observed today, has many members among the peasants but it does not represent the peasants.) He supports strongly the notion that there must be a steady advance in living standards. Socialism must prove itself in the present by getting the gains of productivity to the workers. He argues that the balance of payment deficit should be as large as can be financed. The issue was much in discussion today, for the postponement (equals cancellation) of credits by the U.S.S.R. and East Germany had just been announced. We had a couple of cups of Turkish coffee while we talked. He told me that it took about forty to get him through his daily editorial duties.

Afterward I had more coffee with a young West-

ern-trained intellectual who is not, I would assume,
a party member. He is not very happy, for he finds
his life rather restricted and monotonous. But he
says the inhibiting factor in intellectual expression
is the hierarchial character of the society, and the
stuffiness of those who have arrived, and not punish-
ment of heresy. The latter, he says, is not now a problem. The intellectual life of Belgrade is not very
lively. He feels — one or two others have mentioned
this — that the most serious problem of the country
is discontent and separatism in Croatia. The Croats
feel, as of old, that they are being held back by the
backwardness of Serbia.

Later I had dinner with some American friends.
Present also were the Canadian ambassador and
wife, the Abels of the *New York Times,* and a Yugoslav economist and his wife. However, the discussion
turned mostly on De Gaulle, France, and the United
States. I imagine that some of the world's most intelligent and attractive people work for the *New York
Times.*

Free Money; More Economics

May 30
I had breakfast with some friends from the embassy
and then was taken shopping by Mrs. Stanovnik. I
had told my hosts that I would consider myself com-
pensated by their hospitality — which is indeed all
that could be asked — but I sensed that this was not
entirely satisfactory. They wished to feel that they
were paying me, however modestly. (The question
did not arise in Poland where I was being sponsored
by the Ford Foundation.) So as a solution — since
dinars may not be exported, at least in payment for
nonessentials — I agreed to take modest reward in
kind. A young scholar from the Institute came along
with the official pocketbook. For the first time I had
the experience of spending free money — zero margi-
nal utility. We bought some nice Serbian embroidery
and some silver jewelry. When I had difficulty decid-
ing between two bracelets, I was promptly urged to
take both. So deep is the force of habit, however, that
I found myself impelled to choose.

Then we had the final session at the Institute — a further discussion of the lectures which was both lively and friendly — and then more expressions of thanks and good will. Following lunch with two senior economists I was taken to the airport and passed quickly through the formalities of departure. Certainly, it has been a most pleasant and entertaining week.

I leave with the distinct impression that the "market socialism" of Yugoslavia is a going concern. The clue is in the price system. In Poland nearly all prices are fixed by the state. If the price relatives are not right, then the incentive structure is unreliable. A firm that expands output at a loss — if it happens that its prices are low and its costs high — may be performing a useful service. And the higher the output and hence the higher the loss, the greater the service. The Poles recognize the problem and, as I have noted, they are desperately striving to reform their price structure. But this takes a year or two. By the time it is finished another reform will be needed. There have already been four or five "reforms."

The Yugoslavs solve this problem by leaving about 70 per cent of prices to the determination of the individual enterprise. Not even Belgrade hotel prices are fixed, and as the result of the completion of the

Metropole prices of hotel rooms are coming down. The individual (public) enterprise has the power to adjust its prices, and the problem of price relatives is self-solving — if the prices are too low, the firm can raise them and vice versa. This means in turn that earnings can be used as the test of performance and also that earnings can be partly shared by management and workers as an incentive. The 30 per cent of prices that are fixed include utilities and things like steel or fertilizer where there is a particular interest in the price. Workers' councils, a development of recent years, are also credited with a considerable improvement in the operation of the individual enterprise. All in all the Yugoslav system seems much more flexible and pragmatic than that of the Poles. Clearly, also, it is better designed to incur the disfavor of the Soviets. To the extent that capitalism is identified with free prices and the market, it represents a backsliding to capitalism and capitalist incentives. (No concessions are made or contemplated on the issue of state ownership of the means of production, however.) There is much interest in Yugoslavia as to how far the Poles can go in unwinding their economy without having an ideological conflict with the Russians on this point. The notion that satellite economic policy should follow the "social schematism" of the Russian development

99

seems to me the most dangerous mistake the Soviets are making. Adaptation to the higher living standard, the less self-sufficient character, the nonsocialized agriculture, and the cultural and economic mores of these countries would seem to be an imperative. Indeed, this is the lesson of the Stalinist period. Yet one guesses that the Soviets still believe that ideology as distinct from such "objective circumstance" must be the controlling factor.

The Yugoslavs, incidentally, are completely set in their determination to pursue their own course. Of this there cannot be the slightest doubt. There is a domestic difference between those who would decide economic issues more dogmatically and those who argue with great vigor and pride for flexible and pragmatic socialism. But I did not encounter anyone who was disposed to think that Russian doctrine and experience should be considered the guide. I imagine some such may exist and that I was less than likely to encounter them. But it is hard to believe that they are numerous.

We are approaching the white cliffs of Dover. I am glad that there is nothing about the British economy which at the moment stirs my curiosity.

Economic Power in the American Setting

In the last century the central concern of economists was with the problem of value or price. In this century it has been with the total output of the economy and with the means of increasing it. But closely related to both of these concerns has been the problem of economic power. This question was explicit with Marx. But it was rarely absent from the thoughts of others. Who, or what group, in the society had the power of economic decision? To what extent was it a perquisite of birth? of position? of wealth? To what extent were some individuals subject, in their economic well-being, to the actions, arbitrary or otherwise, of other people? To what extent might the individual's real income be increased or decreased by the decision of some other person concerning the wage to be paid or the price to be charged? To what extent, in a word, did exploitation exist, and how might this be forestalled or prevented? I need scarcely add that much more than mere economic well-being was involved. Economic subordination is rarely consistent with political freedom. The man who is excessively beholden to another for his livelihood will usually be beholden to him for his liberties.

Appendix

As I have noted, the issue of power was explicit in the Marxian system. And perhaps it was because the problem assumed such a portentous form in this system — in the power relationships of the social classes — that non-Marxists were less disposed to debate the issue. It was a disagreeable question. Perhaps some thought that to talk of the power conflict between social classes was to magnify that conflict. So the discussion was muted. In part, the issue was swept under the rug.

This, however, is a poor way of handling issues and certainly not one to be commended to the scientist. In these lectures I am going to talk about the problem of economic power in the American economy — a subject which has long interested me. I would like to ask and seek to answer the question of where economic power resides in modern American society, and to see in what fashion we have come to terms with this ancient problem. My purpose is to discuss the nature of the solution rather than to pass upon its merits. It is my own feeling that, perhaps more by good luck than otherwise, we are on the way to a tolerable solution. It is a pragmatic and, in some respects, an awkward one, and it leaves important unsolved problems. Yet, on the whole, it serves fairly well. But it is no part of my purpose to reflect on this achievement. The task of the social scientist is analysis and not self-congratulation.

Let me first remind you of the historical setting of this problem.

II

In the last century, on one point of importance, there was nearly complete agreement between the Marxian and classical economists. Both agreed that economic power — the power of one individual or group to affect the well-being of another group and hence to abuse or exploit it, could be effectively eliminated from economic life and, indeed, should be eliminated. In the Marxian system, I take it, this was to be the supreme accomplishment of the revolution and the overthrow of the bourgeois. In the classical system the same result was already achieved within the framework of capitalism through the benign agency of competition. Were there competition, no individual or firm had power to do another harm, for this was to his competitive disadvantage. If he overcharged his customer or his suppliers or if he underpaid his workers, i.e., if he exploited either those with whom he traded or those whom he employed, these could go elsewhere. Customers would buy elsewhere; suppliers would sell elsewhere; workers would work for another employer. This right was implicit, for the word *competition* implied the ability to exercise these choices. And, obviously, a man who was without power to damage either his clients or his workers — whose prices and wages were fixed in the common market for these things — was without effective economic power of any kind. The power to do damage was eliminated by eliminating economic power itself.

Such was the competitive model and, in another interesting parallel with the Marxian system, it allowed but a minor role to the state. If competition precluded the misuse of economic power, state legislation for the same purpose was obviously unnecessary and redundant. There was no need for state intervention to enforce desirable modes of behavior, for competition rewarded these also. In the Marxian system the withering away of the state had to await the revolution and the atrophy of acquisitive modes of thought. In the classical system the state was always inconsequential. Marx and Adam Smith had this in common, that the state was central to the enduring society of neither.

In accordance with the well-understood principles of classical international trade theory, which calls on everyone to maximize his comparative advantage, I shall henceforth forego discussion of Marx, on whom I cannot count myself an adequate scholar, and confine myself to the classical or capitalist development. Against the above background of theory, let me suggest something of the larger economic setting in the latter part of the last, and the early part of this, century.

III

In the industrially advanced countries — England, France, Germany, and the United States — the first performer on the economic stage was the industrial entrepreneur. In the nineteenth century he established himself as the dominant figure. Indeed, it was hard to think of him save as the only one. Unions were only gradually and painfully coming into being and asserting their legitimacy. The United States, which lagged behind the other industrial countries in this respect, did not have a strong labor movement until the decade of the nineteen-thirties. Twenty-one years ago this spring Mr. John L. Lewis, then the head of the Steel Workers' Organizing Committee, and Mr. Myron C. Taylor, then the head of the United States Steel Corporation, signed an agreement recognizing the union in the plants of the Corporation. This paved the way for the organization of the steel industry which, in turn, was a decisive step in American trade-union history.

Farmers in the nineteenth century were also unorganized and without power. There was agrarian discontent and agitation. In the latter part of the century the famous Granger movement flashed across the American west, momentarily winning legislative battles, passing laws to control the railroads, trading firms, and the other industrial enterprises by which the farmer thought he was being exploited. But presently the movement subsided as did others that followed it.

The farm organizations lacked the cement that would hold them together for cohesive action. Coöperative selling by farmers, though much discussed and provided with a measure of public sponsorship, developed mostly in rather specialized products and markets, as for fruits and dairy products. In general, it is still confined to these things. Consumers — the public at large whom the economic system was meant to serve — were also amorphous and voiceless. In England and in Scandinavia in the late years of the last century and the early years of the twentieth, the coöperative movement gained power. Consumers banded together to oppose their powers as buyers to the power of those who supplied them. In the United States, with the important exception of the purchase of agricultural supplies, the consumer-coöperative movement did not develop impressively.

So the field remained to the industrial firm. It was a tightly organized, strongly articulated unit under the strong and disciplined direction either of those who owned it or their designated executives. Surrounding it was the powerless population of farmers, white-collar workers, and the public at large. Inevitably, the tightly organized and wholly purposeful business organization made its influence felt on government. In the early part of the nineteenth century in the United States the influence of the agrarian and aristocratic south and the agrarian and democratic frontier was strong. On occasion, it was dominant in the United States Congress and in its influence on the Executive. In the second half of the century, without much question, industrial power was in the ascendency in Washington. Farmers and workers had the majority of the votes. But business firms had the sense of direction and the capacity for action. They also had the money. In the nineteenth century even conservative journals and commentators commented upon the dominance of the larger business interest in the conduct of government.

Appendix

Finally, in the last decades of the last century and the first years of the present century, industrial firms in the United States grew to great size. This was partly in realization of the economies of scale in highly capitalized production. It was perhaps even more the result of mergers designed to "stabilize" competition. Many of the firms now famous on the American scene — United States Steel Corporation, International Harvester, International Paper, International Nickel and (a little later) General Motors all trace to this period. The recurrence of the word *international* in these names suggests the spacious ambitions of the organizers, although in most cases the nation principally involved beyond the borders of the United States was Canada.

In light of these developments the classical model, with its assumption that economic power was dissolved — or at least contained — by competition, became increasingly implausible. The theory still attracted belief, for it was a complete and internally consistent system. And given something that is theoretical, complete, and consistent, economists (and intellectuals generally) have regularly shown a remarkable ability to ignore empirical evidence. Journalists and other commentators, less inhibited by theory, vigorously assailed the economic and political power of the "trusts." In 1913 the United States Congress conducted a lengthy investigation of the bankers or the "money trust," as it was called — it took official cognizance, if you will, of the role of finance capital. Thorstein Veblen, the most original and iconoclastic of American economists, developed his theory of business enterprise in which the business power was constantly preoccupied with curbing or restraining what he termed the "excessive prevalence and efficiency of the machine industry" and hence its tendency to overproduce and endanger profits. The power to restrain or to monopolize output was inherent in this analysis.

Finally, even in the dominant classical tradition, there was uneasiness and unsettlement. This interpretation was not lacking in adaptability and in its capacity to rationalize inconsistent evidence. But one thing was indispensable and that was competition. Monopoly was as objectionable to the classical economist as to Marx. The merger movement and the rise of the great trusts seemed to threaten the very foundations of the system, for the trusts were inimical to competition, and without competition nothing could be defended. These ideas gave to American radicalism some fifty years ago an aspect and attitude which it retains to this day. This includes a deep suspicion, verging at times into hostility, of large business enterprise. It was extended, notably under the leadership of the late Justice Brandeis, to a questioning of the efficiency and even the morality of the large concern. These attitudes were not socialist but the antithesis of socialism. The large firm was regarded as the enemy of classical capitalism. Those who assailed it were defending a theoretically consistent capitalism. Over the last fifty years classical defenders of capitalism have been the most articulate and influential, and at times the most feared, critics of American business.

V

Not many Americans would argue, I think, that in the last thirty years the economy has moved toward the classical model. On the contrary, the statistics affirm a comparatively high (although it is not clear that it is an increasing) concentration of manufacturing, mining, power production, and transportation in the hands of a relatively small number of firms. These matters have regularly been studied by the Federal Trade Commission, an agency of the United States government. For the year 1950 it concluded that, of the 300,000 manufacturing companies in the United States, the largest 1,000 shipped about 55 per cent by value of all goods produced. And the largest 100 firms shipped about 35 per cent. These figures have not gone unchallenged. The FTC, which owes its genesis to the liberal reaction to big business I have just mentioned, has been regularly accused by its critics of exaggerating the extent of the concentration in order to draw attention to the issue. Nonetheless, as a guide to orders of magnitude, its conclusions are valid.

In recent decades economic theory in the classical tradition has also ceased to make a sharp division between competition and monopoly. Between the two are intermediate forms of market organization, most notably oligopolistic market structures, which partake of some of the characteristics of classical competition and some of single-firm monopoly. This notion of a fusing of monopoly and competition has also done much to undermine confidence in the competitive model.

Yet in recent years the issue of economic power, and particularly that of the power of the great corporations, has receded as an issue in the United States. Of this I think that there can be not the slightest doubt. As compared with fifty years ago, it sustains a far smaller amount of intellectual discussion and debate. It is far less the subject of political agitation and debate. It is no longer central to the political program of any party or group. I do not wish to imply that the issue is dead. The presence or absence of competition in markets is still discussed. The enforcement of the anti-trust laws is still debated and vigorously urged. The large corporation is still regarded with misgiving in many quarters — as the heads of these corporations are aware. But elections are no longer fought on these issues. They sustain no strong radical position. In recent months a far more ardently discussed question has been not whether the modern corporation exercises undue power over its workers or customers but whether it insists on too great a conformity on the part of its executives. People have been worrying about what has come to be called the "organization man."

Thus the paradox of our time is that as faith in the classical solution of the problem of economic power has disintegrated so has concern over the issue itself. We can be reasonably certain that this is related to a fairly deeply seated change in American life. Where there is a real source of popular apprehension and discontent, American politicians are almost certainly as skilled as any in seeking them out. The man who wishes to criticize the large corporation is under no effective restraint. His access to the public — especially by way of the unions — is probably better than ever before. Why has this portentous issue sunk into the background? What has been the nature of the solution, if such it may be called?

VI

In part, the solution has been general economic well-being. The years since World War II have been prosperous in the United States. Prosperity is a notable solvent for social tensions. (*Pro tanto*, it is bad for economists. Ours is a strongly countercyclical profession. We thrive on misfortune, at least so long as we are not blamed for it.) In part also this has been a period of diminishing tension because — in contrast, for example, with the prosperous period of the twenties — the share of income accruing to wage earners has evidently been rising. (In 1929 wages, salaries, and other labor income was 59.6 per cent of national income: in 1950–55 it averaged 67.5 per cent.)[1] But this change itself obviously requires some explanation.

By many Americans, the change is explained in terms of a transformation of the personality of the business executive. He is less avidly concerned with the maximization of profits than hitherto. He has become more conscious of his responsibilities to the public. He has become committed to what has come in the United States to be called "good public relations." Thus he no longer uses his power with the aggressive ruthlessness which characterized nineteenth-century capitalism.

I think it fair to say that most social scientists regard this explanation with amused skepticism. Profits are still an important test of performance in our business system. In my own view, in a capitalist society, they should be and must be. And even granting that there has been a transformation of the attitude of the business executive, one would still wish to inquire what brought it about. History has marked some notable transformations in individuals like the Buddha at Sarnath. But most of us are conditioned to mistrust such an explanation when it is applied to a group.

I would note in passing that there has been a change in the character of the business corporation since the nineteenth century. And this may have had some effect. In the great age of corporate entrepreneurship, corporations were characteristically headed by men with a large interest as owners. The power and prestige that were associated with wealth were actively joined with the power that goes with the active direction of a large industrial enterprise. Increasingly, ownership and active management of corporate enterprise have become divorced. In the typical case, the industrial corporation is now headed by a professional executive who has made his way up through the managerial hierarchy in a manner not greatly different from the way an energetic and ambitious man makes his way up through the civil service. While his emoluments are not negligible, his share in the ownership of the enterprise is usually nominal. The old-fashioned entrepreneur, both as director and owner, was able to think of the corporation as the instrument of his personal will. The professional manager cannot do so. His career has conditioned him to think of himself as the servant of the enterprise. In the nineteen-thirties the last of the great automobile companies to recognize the United Automobile Workers and to sign a union contract was Henry Ford. (The personally-owned steel companies also resisted organization the longest.) Ford was not competitively the strongest producer. But he was the only automobile manufacturer who was the owner of the enterprise he headed. In his struggle with the union he needed answer to no one but himself. In the fourth decade of the twentieth century Ford was a rather exceptional figure. In the last quarter of the nineteenth century he would have been a typical one.

VII

However, the most important contribution to the solution of the problem of economic power has come from a different direction. While the classical economists had their eyes fixed on competition — on other participants on the same side of the market — power was being countered from across the market. Those who were subject to economic power had a powerful incentive to organize or otherwise to win bargaining power to protect themselves. This countervailing power, as I have called it, is a self-generating regulatory force — as indeed competition was presumed to be. Power on the one side of the market both creates the need for, and proclaims the existence of rewards to be captured by, countering action on the other side of the market.

The existence of countervailing power must be seen in relation to the evolution of popular government. The modern state is not without a position and a dyamic which is above and apart from its influence by popular pressure. But neither is it remote from such pressures. Among modern governments those of the United States and France must be counted as relatively sensitive to group pressures, just as those of the United Kingdom and Canada are markedly less so. We cannot doubt that in the seventeenth and early eighteenth centuries commercial power, and in the nineteenth century industrial power, made ample use of the state as an instrument of economic goals. In this century, as workers, farmers, and other groups have become politically conscious, active, and powerful, they have turned also to the state. Support that was once sought principally in behalf of commerce or later of industry is now sought on behalf of a plurality of interests. And especially it is sought by those groups which are great in number, and hence in political power, but who feel themselves intrinsically weak in their market position.

Thus the trade unions have sought and won a legal climate basically favorable to themselves. In the industrial states — Michigan, Pennsylvania, New York — where the political power of workers is greatest, their success has also been greatest.

Farmers have felt the disadvantages and experienced the adverse movements in terms of trade, from selling competitively in markets that are often characterized by market power on the buying side. In their case self-organization has been difficult. So they have sought the direct intervention of the state in reinforcing their bargaining position. Of late, American farmers have not been satisfied with the support that the government has accorded to their bargaining position. In recent decades farmers have shrunk from a large to a comparatively small political minority, for while our population has been increasing rapidly, the number of farmers has been showing an absolute decline. And this failure of farmers to win support for their bargaining position is also related to their political situation. However it should be added that shorter-run political influences have also had an effect.

Business power, of course, also remains important in the

American economy and polity. It is the most tightly organized and tactically the most maneuverable of the sources of economic power, and it has marked advantages in placing its case before the public. On the other hand, and this is important given the political context of this solution, workers and farmers deploy the larger battalions.

In England and in Scandinavia the great coöperatives have long exercised a measure of bargaining power on behalf of the consumers. In the United States there has been a similar development of buying coöperatives by farmers. However, general consumers' coöperatives have not been able to get a foothold. Their failure is at least partly because their role had been effectively pre-empted by the mass distributors, as the great chain retailing organizations are called. These organizations have not hesitated to seek out alternative sources of supply or to go into production on their own behalf when they suspected that excessive prices were being charged and excessive profits were being earned by their suppliers. I have argued, subject to a good deal of dissent from my economic colleagues, that this also represents a version of countervailing power. These organizations, in a happy coincidence of self-interest and welfare, have flourished by exercising their formidable market power on behalf of the consumer. No one, I believe, claims that the position of the American consumer would be as favorable in the absence of these mass buyers.[2]

I would not wish to argue that countervailing power emerges as an antidote to every position of economic power. (Many of my colleagues have advanced this as a flaw in the theory while failing to observe that a similar bill of exceptions could always be advanced against competition.) Nor may one suppose that the balance of power is always equal. On occasion, as some anxious critics have suggested, countervailing power may, in some sense, become the more important. It would be foolish to contend that the scales are always level. Finally, as I have been at pains to point out, the juxtaposition of strong corporations and strong unions has left us with a difficult and still unsolved problem of reconciling high employment with price stability.

Nonetheless, the pluralism that is associated with countervailing power seems to me central to the solution — perhaps I should say to the degree of solution — of the problem of economic power which we have found in the United States. Without unions; without a strong political movement in agriculture; without the less dramatic action of other economic groups on their own behalf; without the interaction of these with the state; and without the conflicts which are created within the business structure by the fact that the public rewards with its patronage those who exercise power on behalf of the public, there would be only one focus of private economic power in the economy. That would be the great business organization. This, in turn, would have a decisive influence on the state. Such a distribution — or to speak more accurately, such a concentration — of economic power would scarcely be acceptable to those who were excluded from access to it. Had such a structure, which reflected the tendencies of nineteenth-century capitalism, remained unmodified, it could scarcely have survived. That the excessive concentration of power has within it the seeds of its own destruction is something that evokes the agreement of such diverse philosophers as Marx and Lord Acton.

The American solution is not one of great elegance. I doubt that it will ever make the more precise model builders entirely happy. But, the essential principle, that of the diffusion rather than the concentration of power, is sound. Countervailing power is also based on market relationship, and it is here, in a capitalist society, that the arbitration of group well-being occurs. These facts, and the decline of economic power as an issue, are my reasons for thinking that countervailing power is not without importance, at least in the American setting.

One tradition in economic thought has long sought to divorce questions of economics from those of politics. That this is a highly artificial separation will be conceded by most. But, as I have made clear in this lecture, we have usually thought of politics as the creature of economics. We now see that the reverse can be true. The problem of economic power has been solved because the political society, by its nature, allowed and indeed encouraged people to organize or demand the defenses they required.

An economy that is regulated by countervailing power is not wholly stable — at or near full employment it will have a persistent tendency to inflation. That is because when demand is strong conflict can be resolved not by bargaining but by passing the costs on to the public. It follows that if full employment is to be a goal of economic policy the reconciliation of group interest is one of the inescapable functions of the modern state. It must have machinery for accomplishing this. One imagines this will not be easily designed or operated. This problem we have not yet faced. There is still a tendency to hope that it will solve itself. There are other questions. Yet an imperfect solution of the problem of economic power is vastly to be preferred to none at all. For it was the belief that no solution existed that once led to the confident predictions that capitalism could not survive.

Notes

Warsaw: First Impressions
1. Robert Dorfman, Paul A. Samuelson, and Robert M. Solow; *Linear Programming and Economic Analysis* (New York: McGraw-Hill, 1958).

Tour of Warsaw
1. Professor of economics at Duke University and past president of the American Economics Association.
2. Edward S. Mason, *Economic Concentration and the Monopoly Problem* (Cambridge: Harvard University Press, 1957).
3. Formerly professor of economics at the University of Chicago, subsequently first postwar Polish ambassador to the United States, and now professor in the University of Warsaw and deputy chairman of the Polish Council of State.

Visit to the Country
1. New York banker and assistant secretary of state for economic affairs under President Truman.
2. Douglass Cater has been for several years head of the Washington office of *The Reporter*.

Lecture
1. Gottfried Haberler, professor of economics, Harvard University.

117

Notes

The Polish Economic Society

1. A teaching technique employed at the Harvard Graduate School of Business Administration. It should perhaps be said that not even most friends of the case method would defend it on these grounds.
2. See Appendix.

American Communists; Polish Prices

1. Professor of economics at Stanford University: *The Political Economy of Growth* (New York: Monthly Review Press, 1957).

Cracow

1. Paul A. Samuelson, *Principles of Economics,* 4th ed. (New York: McGraw-Hill, 1958).

Last Day in Warsaw

1. Wassily W. Leontief, *The Structure of the American Economy,* 2nd ed. (New York: Oxford, 1953).
2. James S. Duesenberry, *Income, Saving, and the Theory of Consumer Behavior* (Cambridge: Harvard University Press, 1949).

Warsaw to Belgrade

1. Dr. Janez Stanovnik of the Institute of International Politics and Economics. The Institute, which concerns itself with economic and other developments abroad, was my official host in Belgrade.

More on Agriculture

1. Wassily W. Leontief, professor of economics, Harvard University.

Economic Power in the American Setting

1. Selma F. Goldsmith, "Income Distribution: Changes in the Size Distribution of Income," *American Economic Review,* May 1957.
2. Effective bargaining is, of course, only one of their services. They have, among other things, notably increased labor productivity in this industry.

118